The Life Edit

Get Clarity, Take Back Control and Create
a Fabulous Midlife using Daily Journalling

Sarah Adams

R3THINK PRESS

First published in Great Britain in 2019
by Rethink Press (www.rethinkpress.com)

© Copyright Sarah Adams

Cover image © Shutterstock | azure1

Praise

'If you are ready for a new chapter in your life, one of positive change, growth and fulfilment, then look no further! The LIFE EDIT will help you get there through journalling and inspirational writing. Dare to dream, believe it is possible and follow the guidance in this fabulous book.'
— **Sue Stone**, author and inspirational speaker, The Sue Stone Foundation

'I truly enjoyed this book. The author's enthusiasm and positivity shine through – just like having a chat with her. I had become a procrastinator and will definitely take on board the suggestions. I recommend this book and know several people who I will be buying copies for. I have started journalling every day and I love it.'
— **Nicola Bowen**, landscape gardener

'I love this book – so well written and interesting. Very useful. Bloody brilliant.'
— **Chris Prior**, practice manager

'I loved this book so much. I couldn't put it down and had to make a rule to read to the end of each chapter before stopping. I have a new journal, and I am now starting my own life edit.'
— **Patsy Holmshaw**, financial analyst

'This book is marvellous. It's empowering but witty throughout. The reader knows just enough about the author to know she has earned her stripes. A triumph!'
— **Suzan Croxford**, business owner

Contents

Foreword

If I could give this book as a gift to everyone I care about, I absolutely would as it's changed my life beyond belief. It's an absolute diamond in a sea of well-meaning but often inauthentic inspirational coaching. It's easy to understand, follow and implement and made all the more powerful because Sarah has done all the hard work herself to be able to be such a source of hope.

For years I've battled anxiety brought on by some challenging life events. I'd crucially lost hope and was stuck in a negative thought cycle of being help-less and that nothing would ever change. Following a daily writing routine has genuinely given me back the reins. Just a small investment in myself each day has yielded results I get a bit emotional thinking about – I'm focused, I'm driven and most special of all is that this course has freed up my time to help others. If you spend your days thinking you wish you had more hours to get all the positive stuff done, please read this book. It changes lives because the clever lady at the helm is a caring genius. What's not to like?!

Marianne Shaw, mother of three. Journalist. Cancer survivor. Total legend. Future Prime Minister.

Introduction
Why You Need This Book

In a nutshell: I have written the book that I wished was available twenty years ago when my life took a dramatic and unexpected dive into oblivion. I have used my passion, energy, belief and experiences to create this book and my LIFE EDIT programme. I use it. It works.

It's exactly the book that I and so many other women need right now as we embrace our middle years – our golden years, our hot-to-trot, taking-no-prisoners years, our 'look at us, we are fantastic and we have so much more to offer' years.

If you are now at a flashpoint in your life (perhaps in more ways than one) and feel that your energy needs to be directed into something more positive and fulfilling; if you are stuck at a crossroads and can't see the wood for the trees, wanting to make changes but uncertain of where to go next; or if you feel you are slowly but surely fading into the background and losing your voice, your confidence and your credibility – then this book is for you.

By the time we hit our middle years, we have usually experienced one or more major life events. Far from being a time of 'crisis', this is actually the best time of our lives – a time to embrace our experiences, wisdom and the fact that we no longer have to spend time proving anything to anyone.

The daily LIFE EDIT programme that this book is about can be used to manage, plan and sort out a whole range of topics, ideas and challenges – from reworking your wardrobe to redefining your career, and everything in between:

- Returning to work / changing your career path
- Working from home / becoming self-employed
- Starting a business
- Getting a divorce
- Dating (again)
- Coping with single parenthood
- Coping with bereavement
- Facing financial challenges

- Dealing with health and wellbeing challenges
- Coping with empty nest syndrome
- Updating your home or garden
- Becoming a stepmum
- Improving your self-confidence and self-esteem
- Updating your look
- Gaining better self-belief

And – crucially – exploiting your true potential in midlife.

I have been through all of these and, by some miracle, I am still here to tell the tale. I am a journalist and an accredited and experienced university lecturer, coach and mentor. I also have loads of direct life experience and a bulletproof way to navigate through it all, survive it, thrive on it and come out the other side – with a life designed and created by me, for me, the way I want to live it.

And you know what? You can have all that, too. I urge you to read this book and take up my challenge to change your life in just a few minutes a day over the next twenty-one days.

Using the eight-step LIFE EDIT, you will start to see changes fast by embracing a daily writing routine.

It won't always be easy – there will be awkward questions, pressure, tears – but it will work. It's time to stop feeling invisible, ignored, frustrated, scared and hopeless. It's time to get out from under the duvet, put your big-girl pants on, ditch the Netflix binge and live your best life. And the best bit? There is no naked moon-gazing, tarot cards, mystical spells or chanting, unless you want to. All you need is a lovely new notebook, a pen and an open mind. What's not to love?

Here are the eight steps of the LIFE EDIT that you will go through as you read this book:

1. Let go! Love your life! Get limitless!

2. Inspiration. Ideas.

3. Focus. Fear. Future.

4. Edit. Explore. Evaluate.

5. Embrace empowerment.

6. Delete. Decide. Define.

7. Intentions and integrity.

8. Time to transform.

There is no need to become prisoners of our past. Life shows us lessons, not life sentences. Write sentences that really matter and will make a profound difference; promise yourself that you will live your best life. You have come this far and worked bloody hard to get here – so now it's about you. There are no limits to achieving whatever you want.

As midlife women, we have so much to offer the world – let's make sure we get out there and do it.

So what's it all about, and how will daily journalling and the LIFE EDIT process help you?

It is well documented that keeping a journal or diary, or taking part in regular creative writing sessions, can help us to unravel our thoughts, give us clarity and help us to achieve short, medium and long-term goals that lead to positive changes in our lives. And yet very few of us actually make time to write down our goals. In her Written Goal Study at Dominican University in North Carolina, Professor Gail Matthews asked 149 people to split into five groups. Group 1 was asked to just think about their goals, group 2 were tasked with writing down their goals, the third group had to write down their goals and make action commitments, group 4 had to write down their goals, make action commitments and share them with a friend and the fifth group had to do all of that and send a weekly progress report to a friend.

Those from all groups who wrote down their goals achieved significantly more than those who just thought about them.[1]

---

[1] Gail Matthews conducted The Written Goal Study at Dominican University; https://sidsavara.com/wp-content/uploads/2008/09/researchsummary2.pdf

Through the people I have worked with and the coaching work I have done, I know that those of us who do this achieve great things and make profound and significant changes to our lives, and there is no reason why that should be any different in midlife.

All of us have a 'story' that we tell ourselves about who we are and what our lives are like. We can convince ourselves of almost anything and we can use our story to influence every part of our lives. Although we get genuinely excited by the prospect of change and the idea we can 'have it all', we often have long-held beliefs that success is for other people and we are somehow not worthy. In our middle years, or if we find ourselves in the middle of a big life change, it is easy to convince ourselves that we have run out of steam and no longer have a contribution to make. If you believe the hype around what happens to women in their middle years in particular, you could be forgiven for thinking that we all suddenly become sad, dreary shadows of our former selves, our lives dominated by weak bladders, hot flashes, elasticated waistbands and a rapidly reducing libido.

Some of these things are symptomatic of our time of life – but just because it's called the menopause, it doesn't mean we have to put everything on pause.

I can see no reason why we can't all live life at full speed and be happy – but you have to do the work. You cannot live by someone else's rules – you have to do this yourself, and I know that isn't always easy. We all have people and situations in our lives that will do their best to stop us, but we need to start being accountable to ourselves and getting the support we need to move forward.

Our self-belief system needs to be robust. We have to believe that we can make changes and that we are worth it. This applies at any age, but it's particularly relevant in midlife.

Our minds are great at telling us stories about things we can't do or have in our lives – but by editing our inner story and changing our way of thinking, we can create a new narrative. We don't have to let our old story dictate the next chapters of our lives; instead, we can create a new one that acknowledges past challenges or mistakes, actively allows us to forgive ourselves for anything that is holding us back, doesn't include those self-limiting beliefs and allows us to make positive change by curating new ideas, plans and goals.

What makes you think you can't make changes and live the life that you want? Have you actually tried to make any changes before? What have you tried – really tried – so far?

Settling for second best can easily and quickly become a bad habit – but we can foster new, positive habits that support change. You are allowed to live a happy life! By drawing on our inner resilience, compassion and gratitude we can all nurture our ideas and write new stories in our journals, using the LIFE EDIT programme as a good starting point. Habits can be changed, but we need to be brave.

The major events in my life shaped who I am today and made me decide to train as a life coach, and writing every day has played a huge part in my own life transformation.

When my marriage collapsed in 2000, I was left with two very young children and I was devastated. The whole experience left a lot of damage that lasted for a long time, including ill health, near financial ruin and lack of confidence and self-esteem. Throughout every life event I have experienced, I have written – both for myself and for my sanity, but also from a purely practical perspective; I had no choice but to write, because I worked as a freelance journalist and had to pay the bills.

For more than thirty years I have worked as a journalist – on local, regional and national newspapers, for magazines and in television. During my varied career, I have interviewed thousands of people, many of them celebrating amazing things in their lives, many at their most vulnerable… and many who didn't want to be interviewed at all.

Journalism gave me an incredible insight into the human condition and how people cope with different situations and stages of their lives. For ten years I helped to run a unique community media social enterprise. This project involved working with groups of volunteers – mostly women – from challenging and deprived communities and training them to write and become community journalists. They went on to work on their own community newspapers, go back to college or university, get jobs and make significant changes to their lives.

Our organisation was so successful at helping groups of people to restart their lives that we were awarded national training accreditation, and won a Santander Enterprise Award as well as funding from charities, trusts and Oxford Brookes University to support the valuable work we were doing by encouraging people to write.

As I started to work with more and more people from different walks of life who were facing different challenges, it became clear that by learning to express themselves through words, their lives were changing. Sometimes the changes were quite small; at other times there were major transformations and massive shifts. I saw people who couldn't even look me in the eye become confident and accomplished at writing and at life in just a few weeks.

The results were astounding. Volunteers became confident, capable and in charge of their own lives. They felt proud, and amazed by what they had achieved. Learning to write and having ownership of the process was the key to starting that change.

I have also worked as a manager in a big corporate communications department. My management experience there combined with the training experience at the social enterprise made me enthusiastic about helping people to reach their full potential by using writing as a tool.

Our social enterprise was lucky to have a university as a training partner; my contact there asked if I would be interested in running some personal development planning courses for them.

The rest is history. I started to introduce personal development coaching into the journalism training courses and the results were incredible. I was then asked to work with other groups: women who needed and wanted to make changes but didn't know where to start, recovering addicts who needed a positive life path to keep them focused, and ex-offenders who had to undertake rehabilitation work to restart their lives.

I have used writing to earn my living for my entire career, but I have also used it as a tool to design and create the life that I have today. I know this process can work; I would never have considered sharing this with other people had I not tried it and used it successfully myself.

I created the LIFE EDIT system to help anyone who wants to change careers, start working for themselves, gain confidence, improve their self-esteem, go back to education or simply have some time to re-evaluate, move forward and make space in their life to embrace change.

This personal development process requires commitment and dedication. It needs you to make the space and time to embrace it and give it the investment it deserves. Trust me – it will pay dividends. Within the first few days, you will start to notice changes, shifts and developments that will change your life and help you to realise your ambitions. This is not magic; it is rooted in science and common sense. If you are positive, realistic and have the courage to make edits to your life and write down and define your plans for the future, then you will find that this process will work brilliantly. But in the same way that simply downloading a fitness app won't get you any fitter unless you use it every day, the LIFE EDIT process will not work unless you actually write every day. You have to do the work.

That's my story so far. I'm looking forward to hearing yours and helping you to rewrite your life.

CASE STUDY

Ceri-Jane started using daily journalling to try to reframe some challenging past experiences and find a way to make plans for a better future for herself and her children. Although lacking confidence initially, she found that adopting a new daily writing habit really helped her.

'It has helped me so much by giving me the self-confidence I need to know where I want to go and what I want to do with the rest of my life. I initially thought I wasn't capable of making change.'

Ceri-Jane, single mum of five. Survivor. Destined for amazing things.

Throughout the book you will encounter little sections titled, 'A quick note about...' These are useful bits of information that help to explain things or answer questions that might come up as you work through the chapters and the LIFE EDIT process.

Here's the first one.

A quick note about... diaries, journals, and the LIFE EDIT

Keeping a diary is very useful; it's different from journalling or writing, but it's an equally important activity, one that's useful and productive as part of a wider recorded progress plan. But keeping a diary to schedule appointments and meetings is more of an organisational management process than a chance to write for inspirational life-changing or creative flow. While it is important to plan our weeks and months in advance to make the best possible use of our time, diarising is not about exploring our goals in detail or clearing the inevitable clutter that we have accumulated.

Journalling has had, and continues to have, a massive renaissance. Journalling today is far more than writing in a 'dear diary' style; there are crossovers with scrapbooking, involving the addition of physical materials, objects, drawings and photographs. We use bullet points, lists, poetry and prose to capture a moment in time that we want to cherish or ideas for things that we would like to do. Creative journalling now extends far beyond the written word and an entire industry has grown around it. It is popular, fashionable and helpful, giving enormous pleasure to those who document their lives in this way.

The LIFE EDIT is a different but complementary activity. The programme was created because I saw the effect that daily, focused and intentional writing had on the groups of people I was working with at the time. Daily writing exercises and this process are about moving forward. We all need moments of reflection and daily writing is about giving us those moments as well as setting clear intentions and finding ways to make things happen, one sentence at a time.

Keeping a diary, creative journalling and daily focused writing all have their place and should be celebrated for their individual values and contributions to personal development as well as for their huge collective impact.

In this digital age, we need to pause more often. Any kind of writing or creativity allows us to do just that. Daily writing works because it sets us up for the day ahead, clearing our minds as we let the pen dance across the pages. It brings ideas to the forefront of our minds, is intentional, precise and personal. It feels less like 'work' because we are not bashing away at a keyboard – but it also tells us that we mean business. If you write it, you will do it. If you just think or talk about it then you probably won't.

I love paper diaries and always use one alongside a planner, writing down everything I need to do and dividing up my time accordingly. I have never been a process-driven person, but I acknowledge how important it is to have systems in place; there is no choice but to embrace them. My business is the business of writing and I need organisational tools, just like everyone else. I need apps and digital interference to help me stay organised and on track. I need to be able to share and collaborate with my team and I need a kick in the pants to get things done.

Diaries and planners are designed to be restrictive and controlling; that is their primary function, because we all need to be organised – even creative entrepreneurs like me. Writing in a notebook is a different activity which performs a different function and has a different outcome. Our notebooks are where the magic happens. They are where our ideas are born, taking shape as they flow from our hearts and minds onto the page. Even this book started life as an idea that became a series of sticky notes and postcards and quickly filled several notebooks before it went anywhere near a screen or a keyboard.

To summarise, here are the significant differences between diaries, journals and intentional daily writing:

Diary: A book with spaces for each day of the year in which one notes appointments or information. An official and organised object designed to keep us on track.

Journal: A daily record of news and events of a personal nature. A reflective and passive object.

Writing: The activity or skill or occupation of composing text. An active process that can be used intentionally and specifically.

Why write?

In a super-fast digital world where we rely so much on technology for both business and leisure, surely writing by hand is outdated, outmoded, old-fashioned, clunky, slow and irrelevant?

You may think so, but it is precisely because we occupy such a super-fast, digitally connected age that we really need handwriting.

It's a different process and it creates different outcomes. When we write for work or business, we inevitably use a screen and a keyboard. It can become a chore but its major appeal is the speed at which we can get things done. It's also easy and it looks neat and ordered with perfect spacing, precisely formed letters and uniform straight lines. It's businesslike and fast, especially if you are a speedy typist.

I am not suggesting we shouldn't use keyboards and screens – I need them as much as anyone else – but where's the harm in using writing in a more mindful, absorbing and intentional way? There is an argument for all of us to write by hand more – whether we're engaged in a planning process for our business, making plans for the rest of our life, planning a specific project or just seeking clarity and focus. Life is about progress and moving forward; intentional writing can play a major part in that process. As our brains and cognitive functions continue to accelerate rapidly towards overload, we need to press pause; when we write by hand, we have to consciously think about what we are doing and how we form the letters, and there is no room for all that external noise.

Having unlimited access to so much incredible (although not always strictly credible) information is amazing and useful, but we need to install a filter. We don't need to be on 24/7 to feel part of something and we don't need to be constantly updated to live in the moment. What we do need is to switch off the white noise, quieten the internal chatter and focus on ourselves, our projects, our businesses and our lives. It is time to remember what we are really here for, what's important and the contribution we can make. We can do all that with a daily writing habit.

PART 1

WORDS OF INSPIRATION

In the first part of this programme, you will get ready to take on the exciting twenty-one-day, eight-step LIFE EDIT challenge to transform your life through daily writing sessions – wherever you are and whatever you are dealing with. You will find out how and why writing helps our self-development, gives us the chance to reframe and focus and create a clear pathway for the way forward. Whatever you want to do next with your life, I promise that writing can help you.

1

Before We Begin

How can this book help you to become the best possible version of yourself and embrace all that midlife has to offer?

This book and the eight-step LIFE EDIT programme have been created to help you make significant changes to your life and to change your outlook and mindset in just twenty-one days by acquiring new, positive habits every day to help you reach your goals.

Together we will edit and write a new life that you design.

Your new life is just 504 hours away!

Before you go any further on this exciting journey of self-discovery and self-improvement, I urge you to pause and answer these questions:

- Are you ready to change your current life and move towards something new and exciting?

- Are you ready to take responsibility for setting your goals?

- Do you know that if you don't act, nothing will change?

- Do you want to move from talking about your plans to actively pursuing them?

- Are you ready to put yourself high on your priority and values list?

- Are you committed to living a more purposeful life?

If you answered 'yes', then you're ready to start achieving your goals. I'm thrilled that you are here – and the best of luck.

Daily writing instructions

To get the most out of this programme, it's important that you complete each writing task. These will be found where you see the word **Write**.

You should also adopt your first new habit, which is to commit to writing for twenty minutes each day for the next twenty-one days.

Writing exercises

Every day you should write down in detail:

1. Your thoughts and feelings about what your life is like now, what you would like to change and why

2. Your ideas and fears about midlife and what the future holds

3. Everything in your life that you are grateful for

There are also specific writing exercises in each chapter that will supercharge the process of making creative space to move forward. Complete them in your journal as you work through the book.

This is a process that should stay with you for life. Each chapter of this book starts with a section that clearly tells you exactly what you will learn and at the end of each section there will be writing actions, tips and hacks. I want you to use this book as a manifesto, a guide and a plan for the rest of your life – starting right now.

Use your journal to track your progress, set your goals and remind yourself how far you have come. Acknowledging your progress is really important but it's something that many of us never actually do because we are too busy racing for the finish line.

I want to help you reach important goals and achieve a positive balance in your life by giving you a way to make a fresh start and get the life that you really want. Just because you are in the middle of your life, there is no reason why you can't harness your experience, passion, knowledge and skills.

Whatever happened in the past is over, and you can't change it. What you can do is learn from it. You can move forward with positive plans to become the best possible version of yourself, and write your life the way you want it to be – your ideas, your script and your vision for your future – and all through the mighty power of the pen.

We will look in detail at how you can take control and plan to make positive changes in the next stage of your life, while reframing and refocusing it in a way that is enriching and ultimately life-changing.

This is a great opportunity to invest time and energy in your greatest resource and asset: you. The next few weeks will be exciting, interesting and exhilarating, as we work together to create plans for whatever you really want to achieve.

You will be given the skills, tools and guidance you need to help you make a fresh start, working towards your important goals and changing your life to be purposeful and fulfilled. You will learn how to value yourself as a priority, and about the importance of making a contribution to you, your family, your friends and the wider community.

This method uses daily writing and journalling, which have been proven to support significant and long-lasting positive change and assist with setting achievable and realistic goals.

The research by Gail Matthews at Dominican University that focused on how goal achievement is influenced by writing goals, demonstrated how by writing down goals, holding ourselves accountable and committing to a regular writing habit we can make positive changes.

By the end of the twenty-one days you will have adopted the eight-step LIFE EDIT method to move forward and achieve your goals. I hope you will use this method for the rest of your life, and will suggest it to friends and family who might also be feeling a bit stuck. I urge you to share the concept and support other people.

How does it work?

Creative processes have been proven to be valuable and effective at helping us to reach our goals, wherever we are in our lives and whatever we are facing.

In his book *Opening Up By Writing It Down*, James Pennebaker – the originator of expressive writing – looks at how writing in this way improves health and eases emotional pain.[2] He says that writing can clear the mind, help with problem solving and enable us to take on new information.

Writing plans down on paper helps to keep us motivated and on track. You will achieve greater success if you start using your journal now to plan your goal-setting and record your thoughts, feelings and any obstacles that come along. We will look at your journal each week to see how your plans are progressing.

By the end of this process you will have:

- Adopted a new daily habit of goal-setting, planning and keeping a journal

- Adopted a new habit of writing down all you are grateful for, every morning and evening

- Learned how to edit your life to make room for positive growth and change

- Curated what is important to you and understood how these things can support you as you move forward to build your team of champions

- Decided and defined your SMAART goals

---

2   James W Pennebaker and Joshua M Smyth, 2016, *Opening Up By Writing it Down: 3rd Ed.* (New York: The Guilford Press.)

- Created positivity and inspirational outcomes by taking specific actions

- Started a new chapter and created a new vision for your story

Get ready to write

For this process to bring you the maximum benefits, it is important to spend some time preparing yourself mentally, physically and emotionally before you start. Having a calm and uncluttered creative clearing that you can use every day as you write in your journal is crucial. In an ideal world you need a space that can be easily kept clear of clutter, has good natural light and is airy, spacious and peaceful. We can't all have a shepherd's hut at the bottom of the garden or a bespoke Romany caravan in an orchard where we can squirrel ourselves away and let our creative juices flow without fear of interruption – but for this process to be truly effective, a creative clearing or space is vital. I urge you to do this as you will find your daily writing challenge difficult without a clear space to do work in.

Maybe you can clear a corner of your favourite room in your home. All you need is a table and a comfortable chair so that you have somewhere to sit and rest your book. If you don't have a window and it's a little gloomy, add a vase of flowers or a potted plant and some LED lights or a candle or two to cast a relaxing glow. A spare bedroom can easily be converted into a creative space – and clearing anything, whether it is physical 'stuff' or emotions, is a critical first step in moving forward. Perhaps clearing an area of your home will be your very first step on this personal development journey. If your own home really isn't an option because it needs major decluttering, then deal with that first. I am not a professional declutterer but there are plenty of people out there who can help you with what can be an emotional process.

Perhaps your life is in a state of flux at the moment and you are living in shared or temporary accommodation where peace and quiet are simply never going to happen. In that case, make use of local coffee shops, libraries, parks (on a nice day, obviously!) and other community spaces. Use earbuds to block out irrelevant noise and listen to calming music as you write.

The key to all this is to not let anything stop you. Yes, there may be challenges in finding a physical space, but you must make every effort to do it.

Preparation for anything new is key to making the most of it and getting the maximum benefit. There are things that you will need before you begin. Check out this shopping list and gather together:

- A new, hardbacked, quality journal, ideally with unlined, acid-free pages. It should be hardbacked because it's going to get a lot of use and needs to be tough! Unlined pages are good because your creativity can flow effortlessly. Make sure you love it. Spend time choosing one, hold it in your hand, smell the paper, feel the cover. You are holding the next chapters of your life right there in your hand. The potential that journal holds is massive. It's exciting.

- A supply of smaller, lightweight, softback notebooks. These are useful for keeping in your bag or car to make notes during the day that you can transfer to your journal later.

- A supply of good pens and pencils. Choose a good pen as your journalling pen and keep it for that purpose – it's worth investing in a decent one. Try a few out before you buy one because it is really important that your primary pen is comfortable to hold and weighted properly. Again, it will be getting a lot of use and will become your new best friend.

- A selection of other pens and pencils for note-taking.

- A pencil case – ideally something sophisticated, grown-up and good quality.

Finally, you will need an open, positive mindset and the determination to make change and write your way to a new life. Procrastination is not your friend. You owe it to yourself to do this properly and professionally. You have already bought this book and read this far so I think it's fair to say: you've got this.

WRITE

Note to Self

- Writing by hand is a much slower process than typing on a keyboard and we are all in a massive hurry to share our every thought on social media.

- As an experiment, try writing a note to yourself, explaining what you are doing and why.

- Describe how you feel right now about choosing to follow this programme. What are you hoping to gain from it? What changes do you envisage in the next twenty-one days? How do you really feel about this stage of your life? Are you scared? Do you feel sad? Confused? Or are you actively embracing all that life has to offer?

- Spend time now writing the answers to those questions and see how you feel afterwards.

- Remember to:
    - Focus your mind on the task, breathe and turn off the tech.
    - Notice how it feels to hold the pen.
    - Think about how different writing on paper is to typing on a keyboard.

Summary

- You should now understand how this programme works and be ready for the next step

- You should have had a go at writing by hand, exploring how you really feel and documenting what is going on right now in your life

- You have checked the shopping list and tips for making sure you are prepared

2
E.X.P.L.O.R.E.

You have done the first writing task as a brilliant warm-up to what lies ahead. Now you can make a proper start on your new daily writing regime using the EXPLORE formula.

This formula breaks down the first stage of your life coaching and daily writing journey into seven fast, easy steps and prepares you to embed a daily writing habit in your schedule.

EXPLORE stands for:

- **E**mbracing daily writing as an effective self-development tool
- e**X**citement about the possibilities that lie ahead

- Planning to write every day; adopting a Positive attitude

- Letting go of self-limiting beliefs

- Owning the process

- Relaxing and writing to clear your mind and make your plans

- Enjoying it!

Let's look at each part of the process in a bit more detail so that you fully understand how important preparation is to the success of this programme.

Embrace daily writing; make this non-negotiable. It is a scientifically proven way to make effective and long-lasting change. The time you spend on your daily writing exercises will never be wasted. Remember this is an important investment in how you experience midlife and beyond. You owe it to yourself to invest in your future.

Everyone can plan to find ten minutes a day to make a start. Commitment is crucial. If you really want to make changes and live your best life, you will – if you commit to it. A daily or weekly planning session will help you get on top of anything that needs to be dealt with and give you a regular routine.

Plan to win. Prepare to win. Expect to win. Embrace positivity.

It doesn't matter how much anyone – including me – tells you that you can achieve greatness, happiness and a life filled with abundance; if you don't believe it, it won't happen. Let go of any self-limiting beliefs that are hanging around. Tell yourself you can do whatever it is you plan to do. Adopt a positive approach to this process and you will see astonishing results. Midlife gives us all the power and strength to make progress. I guarantee that you are a master at telling other people how brilliant they are – but when it comes to you, it doesn't work in the same way. How do I know this? Because I can be just like that, too.

Dedicating specific time to work through the LIFE EDIT programme will have great impact but you must own this right from the get-go. This means adopting it as a crucial part of how you move forward. Being scared or sceptical, having doubts or disbeliefs, will not serve you well. This is your time for change! You have worked hard, maybe raised a family and now as you approach this new and exciting phase it is important to remember: you are allowed to do this.

Being able to relax while you write every day will foster a healthy attitude to your new regime. If it gets stressful, you are unlikely to feel the benefits, so make sure you approach your daily writing time in the right way – every day.

If you enjoy something, then you not only look forward to it, but you become good at it very quickly.

You will want to do it more frequently and you will see results faster.

I did not create this programme to be a chore – in fact, the exact opposite is true. I created it so that anyone can participate and see results fast. This is not about you slaving for hours in a dark corner with only the flickering light of a single candle for company, like a writer from hundreds of years ago. Writing each day should not feel like a punishment.

We cannot change the beginning of our story, but we can start today and create a new ending.

WRITE

- Spend some time now working through the EXPLORE process to make sure that you have the right mindset to make a positive start. Write in your journal how you feel about taking part in the process and be honest about how ready you are.

Fear of failure is a big stumbling block for many people. We see talk as cheap – throwaway, disposable – and if it suits us, we can always manipulate our memory of a particular conversation to cover our tracks, change our opinion or protect our dignity. As soon as we commit to writing down our ideas there is a record, in black and white. The action of transferring messages from our heads and hearts to a notebook is powerful and that is why the LIFE EDIT works so effectively.

CASE STUDY

A daily writing routine can be constructive, gentle and confidence-building at any age, as Elaine discovered when she started to make space each day to write.

'At times in life – such as going through divorce or bereavement – you can easily lose the plot, and the confidence and certainties in the direction you thought your life would take, and where you want to be, change. Life has a way of surprising and shocking us with circumstances we hadn't anticipated and this can make us feel worthless and hopeless. Daily writing has filled my future with confidence and positivity. I am now moving in the direction of a positive and fulfilled life and the sessions have given me the boost that I badly needed to get back on track.'

Elaine, super grandma. Retired scientist. Brilliant calligrapher and accomplished gardener.

Summary

- In this chapter we looked at how daily writing can help us achieve new things in our lives

- We examined why writing and journalling are so effective as part of a new routine to support our self-care and self-development

- We looked at the EXPLORE process and made sure we are ready to write

3
The Power Of The Pen

Keeping a daily journal has never been such a popular tool for supporting self-improvement programmes.

In this chapter, we will look at how powerful daily writing can be, and how writing down our thoughts, dreams and aspirations can help us to manifest changes in our lives. How is writing a tool for change and a way to crystallise the contribution that we want to make as we embrace midlife? Why is it so effective?

We can all talk about things we would like to change, but the physical action of writing something down immediately gives it gravitas and permanence. It draws our attention in a way that spoken words may not. It won't get lost in the ether or in translation.

By documenting how we feel and what we want to change, we are likely to have many 'aha' moments during our personal development journey.

For example, listing all the important areas of our lives and describing in detail what they look like and how we feel about them can have a profound impact on the effectiveness of our editing exercise. Start to think about some aspects of your life that you would really love to transform in the next twenty-one days.

The LIFE EDIT process starts with letting go of self-limiting beliefs and then exploring, editing and clearing so that we have clarity and space to make plans and move forward. Using writing as a tool, we document how we feel about each area of our life as we go through the process.

People who have used this process tell me it's cathartic, therapeutic and calming. It is also loaded with emotion – some positive and some negative – but everyone agrees that writing down how they really feel about every area of their life is hugely beneficial, even though they often find it hard to start with.

In the workshops that I run, the initial part of the process proves to be incredibly powerful and an effective catalyst for change.

The act of giving participants a new notebook and pen and insisting they make time every day to sit and think about their lives and write about them frees them from past mistakes, feelings of guilt and self-limiting beliefs. It gives them the realisation and understanding that what has happened before does not have to dictate the future. It gives them precious time each and every day to examine their lives, and the chance to be honest about what they want.

They tell me they feel as if they have finally been granted permission to be honest about who they are, how they feel about their lives and what they really want from their futures, rather than being made to live the life that someone else thought they should. And it all starts with a pen and a notebook – something simple that they always had access to, but had never thought for a minute would have such transformative power.

The editing and clearing process alone saw them writing pages of notes about how they felt about each area of their life. They then took it one step further, making lists and mind maps of what they needed to change, get rid of or ignore from their past to help them move on. From that came plans for the future. Using colour added to their creative expression and they relished the opportunity to create inspiration and vision boards incorporating powerful, dynamic words and images.

They worked together and supported each other in their weekly writing tasks. They worried that their writing would not be good enough, they stressed

---

about spelling and grammar. I assured them that none of these things mattered – they were free to write however and whatever they wanted. The fact that their writing would never be judged or edited gave them the ultimate freedom and power to access their true feelings and to let their creative flow dictate how they would make positive, lasting changes to their lives.

The power of the written word reaches parts of our hearts and minds that talking alone cannot. We should all be encouraged to embrace writing – at any stage and age – whatever our educational abilities or previous experience. It is a fact that unless a goal is written down there is only a slim chance that it will ever be anything other than a dream.

There are many different styles of personal development journals and notebooks available, all designed to help us map the next stages of our lives while drawing on our creativity.

But the LIFE EDIT method is about far more than just buying a shiny new notebook and making a few random notes every now and then. This is about adopting a new habit that becomes part of your life and changes it almost immediately. It is based on research that proves writing with a pen on paper is a powerful and effective tool for lasting, positive change.

You may be sceptical. How exactly can writing and the creative process shift our belief systems to the extent that our confidence improves and our lives become fulfilling and purposeful? Surely this is all just writing and doodling? You might even view indulging in creative processes as an ideal distraction to throw us off course, mask any challenges we are facing and stop us moving forward – in other words, nothing more than creative procrastination.

But once we start to align writing and creativity with the creative visualisation techniques that are relied upon by wildly successful sports people, business people and public speakers – to name a few – the benefits of it can be seen clearly.

The fact is that within the life coaching and personal development process, a lot of writing, recording, research and planning is done in journals and notebooks, making it an ideal way to edit self-limiting thoughts and beliefs and to set goals. We write, edit, curate and create our lives one sentence at a time – which may sound slow and laborious, but is actually a fast way to see changes.

Even by writing lists we set an intention, a desire and a reminder that something is important enough to be added to that list. Completing tasks gives us a feeling of satisfaction and a renewed and positive outlook as we work towards our next goal. Daily writing can help you achieve whatever you want to do; maybe you have a big business or career goal in mind, or plans to make improvements in other areas of your life like your health and wellbeing? Perhaps you want to write a book, travel the world or have financial freedom? Whatever your next move, I guarantee that a daily writing practice will help you.

WRITE

- In your journal, write down just one thing that you would like to achieve this year and why. What difference will it make to your life? How achievable is it right now? Describe what you want in detail and explore why you have not already done it. What would have to change immediately to start making it a reality?

CASE STUDY

Staying motivated when we start something new can be hard, especially if we don't see results quickly. For Kinga, a daily writing habit really kickstarted her plans for the future.

'I finally feel positive and happy. Taking part in the programme has helped me see my life in a more positive way. I now have a clear outline about what I want to do with my life. I am motivated and believe in myself. Taking part in daily writing sessions has given me motivation to make change.'

Kinga, gorgeous. Ambitious. Hilarious. Happy.

Summary

In this chapter we have learned:

- How powerful daily writing can be and that how you write doesn't matter

- That having the freedom to express ourselves and explore our thoughts and feelings is what really matters

- How even a simple list can start to help us cope better with challenges

4
Be A Goal Achiever

Writing is not new. It has been used for ever to communicate, document, describe, and plan.

It is useful, beautiful and essential. It has the power to entertain and inform, educate and empower, inspire and fascinate, shock and surprise. It can make us laugh, reduce us to tears and help us sort things out in an instant.

In this chapter, we will look at the impact of daily writing and why writing your plans and goals down gives you a huge chance of actually achieving them. You guessed it – it's the science bit.

In its most basic function, writing helps us remember what we need to do, tell people we love them or are thinking about them, and enables us to learn and discover. Writing is a truly amazing thing we all have access to that costs very little. For the cost of a piece of paper and a pen we have the power at our fingertips – and nibs – to change our lives, one word at a time. But despite its beautiful simplicity and enormously powerful ability to create incredible change, few of us ever bother to hand-write much. With keyboards and blinking screens so present in our lives, writing by hand as a human communication tool is being ignored and forgotten.

Although journalling is growing in popularity, I am staggered by how few people use a paper diary or send a physical greetings card any more. With a few taps, you can upload a digital image onto a predesigned template, edit the text, add an address, pay by PayPal and send it to someone, all from the relative comfort of your chosen digital device. Job done. But where is the passion, the emotion, the thought process, the feeling of having created something? You can't hold it in your hand, admire it or add a big lipsticky kiss.

Does it have the same impact as a handwritten card? Hardly ever. The digital process makes 'writing' just another chore, something to be ticked off your list and then disregarded.

The results of the LIFE EDIT prove that the physical act of writing is an impactful method of editing, curating and creating new lives, new plans and new ambitions. It allows us to get rid of anything that is holding us back and to collect the people and things we need to help us move forward. It helps us create the life we want to live.

As you are now taking a few minutes a day to focus on your self-development writing, you will be writing down goals for the future and all that you are grateful for, as a reminder of how much good you already have in your life.

Bookending our day by writing down three things we are grateful for gives us better days of inspired activity and better nights of sleep. Constantly checking social media feeds before bed does not offer the same soporific effect – in fact, the impact on our health and wellbeing is quite the opposite.

In 2007, a study by British psychologist Richard Wiseman PhD proved that almost 90% of people who make New Year resolutions fail to stick to them.[3] Part of the reason is that they didn't write anything down or make a recorded plan. Daily writing helps you to meet your goals by breaking them into manageable and achievable mini- and even micro-goals and also records your progress so far.

---

3   Richard Wiseman PhD, The New Year Resolution Project
      www.richardwiseman.com/quirkology/new/USA/
      Experiment_resolution.shtml

Exactly what is the science behind the power of pen and paper? How is it that two such simple objects and one simple action can create such incredible effects?

The strength and power of writing stems from the fact that it's the primary basis upon which communication, history, record-keeping and art are founded. Writing is the framework of our communication system and punctuates every part of our lives in one way or another.

We encounter writing in many forms and often dismiss its importance and the way it helps us; we are used to seeing memos, agendas, reports and restaurant menus. We disregard its simple energy and ability to motivate us to do mundane things, but if we all used writing more as a self-development tool we would see astonishing results.

Writing is incredibly pliable; you can use it to give information or an opinion, ask a question or write creatively to create poetry or literature. Written words can take a bounty of forms. The words you use can show who you are as a person and the things writing has done in the world are profound. I cannot personally imagine a life that didn't involve writing in one way or another and I am happiest when I am actively engaged in writing projects – whatever they may be.

Although we inhabit a world of information technology with screens and keyboards as our primary 'writing' tools, handwriting still has an important role to play. The most important binding contracts and agreements are still written and signed by hand. Writing is also part of any creative project, whether it is a film, the design of a building or a piece of literature. Without writing, the flow of ideas halts sharply beyond the initial creative source. Ideas and concepts simply never grow.

I amassed dozens of notebooks, bits of paper and postcards with notes and ideas on – along with a plan, a mind map and lots of lists that I wrote entirely by hand – before I went anywhere near a keyboard to write this book.

Writing also entertains us and has intrinsic creative value. We can delve into our subconscious mind to create everything and anything we want – from fantastic imaginary creatures and characters to entire worlds and ultimately the life that we want to live. We can convert daydreams into reality. Documenting our dreams, thoughts and ideas in this way gives us perspective and a feeling that our ideas have permanence and may actually become reality.

I have seen for myself through people I have worked with that writing can help us to think better, plan more effectively and perhaps even improve our intelligence. In the same way that dreaming can fire our imagination, writing allows us to curate our random, scattered thoughts and ideas and edit them into a single beam of useful, impactful information. It opens up a new dimension for the mind to occupy and creates a space for expression and imagination, giving us unrivalled opportunities for ideas, goals and plans to be made, formed and achieved. The sense of satisfaction that writing offers is overwhelmingly awesome.

Science suggests that writing makes us smarter. Studies show that old-fashioned pen-to-paper writing leads to improved cognitive ability, whereas typing skills do not have the same results.

A study in the US that compared the different brain processes used for handwriting and typing found that there are cognitive benefits to putting a pen to paper. These findings give support to the continued teaching of penmanship and handwriting in schools.

Children who don't learn the skill of handwriting may be missing out on an important developmental process. Writing with one hand uses more complex brain power than using two hands to type letters on a keyboard.

The American research project attempted to differentiate between handwriting and keyboard writing and examined their different implications for children's learning and also looked at adults' reading and writing behaviour and experiences. Earlier literature on various writing methods and their implications showed a significant difference between handwriting and the use of a mechanised device. Neuroscientists have noted that the shift from handwriting to mechanised or technical writing has serious implications for cognition and skill development.

There are two aspects of writing: the visual aspect and the perception/motor aspect, otherwise known as 'haptics'. Some studies have revealed that in the actual act of writing by hand you must use your motor skills to copy a letter graphically, a slower process that actually aids in cognitive development.

Writing is a process that needs an integration of visual, motor and cognitive or perceptive parts in order for it to be effective. Perception allows one to remember the shape of the letters to be written while vision and motor skills enable the writing.

When we write using a keyboard, we change this pattern. For example, typewriting involves both hands while handwriting involves one, and handwriting is slower and more laborious than typing. Handwriting requires you to shape a letter, where typing does not.

Some Japanese studies have shown that repeated handwriting aids in remembering the shapes of letters. One study showed that when children learned

words by writing, they remembered them better than
if they learned by typing.[4]

It is clear that good old-fashioned writing with a pen
and paper has profound effects on our cognitive and
intellectual abilities. Surely, then, it is obvious that it's
something we all need to do more of.

Whatever our age, we can all benefit from a daily
writing practice. Above all, writing is an enjoyable
and relaxing thing to do. It's time to forget about your
preconceptions and start afresh with a new attitude to
this simple but powerful art form. Writing can change
your life – if you let it.

Only a small proportion of people bother to write
down their goals and plans for the future. Those of us
who do it achieve great things. Make sure you are one
of those people.

It really doesn't matter how neat your writing is. Just
allocate time each day to reaffirm your goals and edit
out anything that you no longer need or believe will be
helpful to you. Setting goals and writing them down
kick-starts the part of your bran called the reticular

---

4   Associate Professor Nonaka Tetsushi (Kobe University Graduate
     School of Human Development and Environment) looked at the devel-
     opment of writing skills in Japanese children: see www.sciencedaily.
     com/releases/2017/06/170630105033.htm; a 2012 study led by Karin
     James, a psychologist at Indiana University, into the developmental
     benefits of writing by hand can be found here:
     www.lachsa.net/ourpages/auto/2017/2/6/35994471/2%20AP%20
     articles%20on%20psychology%202017.pdf

activating system (RAS). This controls mental agility and alertness and acts as a filter. It edits out anything that is not needed and edits in anything that is.

Writing down your goals is a way of training your brain to recognise what you need and what you don't; this is important, because our RAS presents us with opportunities and resources that support those plans and goals. When we are aware of what we want to work towards, we take positive, inspired actions to get there. The process of writing every day supports that process.

By now, you will have realised that the simplest way to start the process of manifesting change in our lives is to start writing down our goals – daily.

Daily writing habits are the key to:

- Staying focused
- Setting a clear intention that you want to make changes to your life
- Manifesting change by paying attention to your reticular activation system
- Investing in yourself

Your daily writing practices don't have to be an exercise in perfectionism and should never be a chore. Writing is a simple exercise – but don't be fooled by its simplicity. It has a tremendous ability to make us think carefully about our lives; what we want to keep and what we definitely want to change.[5]

WRITE

For five minutes, write fast about how you are feeling. Don't edit. Just write.

- We become pretty adept at hiding our true thoughts and feelings from ourselves. Free writing is a great way to let go and begin the process of exploring and articulating what we really think and feel. Our feelings – both positive and negative – are messages sent to us to show us what is working well in our lives and which things need to change. We just need to make sure we are paying attention.

List four things you think you need to clear from your life.

- Clutter slows us down and stops us making progress. It takes many forms, both physical and emotional. To move forward and create the life we would really love, we need to spend some time clearing and curating our lives. Daily journalling is the number one way to examine your life and challenge any self-limiting beliefs that are holding you back. Isn't it time you created space for exciting changes to happen?

---

5   Gregory Ciotti wrote in *Psychology Today* about how writing makes you happier and smarter: www.psychologytoday.com/gb/blog/habits-not-hacks/201408/how-writing-makes-you-happier-smarter-and-more-persuasive

List three things you are grateful for.

- When we are trying to make changes, it is all too easy to focus on the lack in our lives rather than the abundance. As well as writing down goals for the future, take time every day to acknowledge all that you are grateful for, as a reminder of how much good you already have in your life. Be in the moment, enjoy what you already have, and even better things will start to happen.

Write down two things you would really love to achieve or change in your life.

- We all have hopes, dreams and ideas about how we would like our life to be, but very few of us ever take the time to write them down. By making time to write every day, you have the power to make transformational changes in your life. You will be amazed at the opportunities that present themselves once you channel your energy, focus and positivity into what you really want through daily writing.

Write down one big goal you really want to smash this year.

- A goal is a dream with a plan. When it comes to visualising our future and setting goals, writing is phenomenally powerful. People who write down their goals according to studies are over 40% more likely to achieve them than people who just think or talk about them.[6] Your chances of succeeding are even greater when you also have a detailed written action plan and can describe the success you desire in vivid detail.

---

6 Professor Gail Matthews conducted The Written Goal Study at Dominican: https://sidsavara.com/wp-content/uploads/2008/09/researchsummary2.pdf

Remember:

- Writing is important – it has the power to change everything.

- Writing can make us smarter and more focused. It can help us feel more in control.

- Writing our goals and aspirations down will help us achieve great things.

Be part of that group who *do* write their goals down and get ready to receive positive changes.

Writing actively nurtures the creation of change. For it to work for us, we must acknowledge its power and not be scared of it. We may need to acknowledge the need for some initial editing to free us from past negative experiences of writing and to enable us to see it in a positive and inspiring way rather than as a chore.

CASE STUDY

Finding time in our busy schedules for anything new can be challenging; this is especially true if we have family responsibilities. For Sophie, making the time to write every day had to be non-negotiable.

'Having to commit to writing every day for twenty-one days was not something that I ever thought I could do. I now can't imagine not doing it. It has helped me immensely. I have clarity and a plan for the future and have already achieved some of my goals.'

Sophie, fitness champion. Successful entrepreneur. Mum of two. Financial genius.

Summary

- By adopting a simple daily writing habit that takes up no more than ten minutes, we can make writing our friend and our biggest cheerleader for change

- By gradually increasing our writing time and introducing new writing tasks and exercises, we become more confident and start to see and feel changes

- This will be the start of our new life, if we become a person who writes down their goals

5

The Five Most Important Questions To Ask Yourself

When we write down our goals, ideas and plans for the future, we are starting the creation of a life plan. In this chapter, you will ask yourself some searching questions and really get to grips with some fast writing exercises. To get started, we're going straight into a writing exercise.

WRITE

Ask yourself these five questions and write the answers in your journal:

What has worked well for me in the last twelve months?

- Think about this in detail – what successes and wins have you really experienced? Go back through your diary or calendar. I guarantee you will be surprised at how many positive outcomes there have been.

What do I want to experience in life?

- You are in your prime! Our midlife can be our best life. Explore what you want to experience next.

How do I want to grow?

- Think about you! What do you want to see, learn or do?

Would I be happy if my life were the same in twelve months' time?

- Take time to examine your life as it is now. Just because we get used to living our life in a certain way doesn't mean we have to keep on doing it.

What needs to change?

- The big one. What actually needs to change to help you make a midlife transformation?

These are questions we should all ask ourselves regularly, taking time to formulate answers and ways to support what we want to do next. They can form the basis of a new life plan that gives us the opportunity to craft all the details of what we will do and how – what we want to be, to do and to have in our lives.

By taking time to be peaceful, calm and in the moment, our creativity is ignited and we can more easily visualise positive outcomes.

Spend time writing in your journal about what you want to be, to do and to have, as well as what you want to give and create in your life. What differences will these things bring to your life when you achieve them? Start writing in the present tense as if you are already living your best, most ideal life and see how different it makes you feel. If you're ready for a make-over, or you want to change jobs, upgrade your house, plant a new garden, get fitter or start a new hobby, write it down and add in lots of detail about what you want to achieve.

WRITE

- In your journal, write down ten things that make you feel good about yourself. What are you good at? What do friends and family say about you? What strengths lie beneath? Examining our strengths and any challenges will help us to create a robust life plan.

Losing sight of who we really are is easily done – our lives are busy and ever-changing, but by focusing on everything that is positive about us we are able to read back what we have written about ourselves and appreciate our value and the contributions we can make to our own progress and to other people. By focusing on this list every day, adding to it and editing it as part of the writing process, we can access our powerbase of unlimited self-belief. When things are not quite going according to plan, it's always useful to stop, pause and write down everything about you and your life that is positive. Trust me: plenty of things are working well – you just haven't noticed them yet.

You are amazing

It's useful to create a list detailing how amazing you are. This is difficult and often met with resistance by people who find it uncomfortable even to think of themselves like that, let alone commit it all to paper. But overcoming this barrier (and accepting that this isn't about showing off) helps us to work on those limiting self-beliefs that can prevent us from reaching our goals. By documenting our strengths and celebrating our successes, we are writing our life – past, present or future.

Writing a weekly action plan is an important component of a life edit. This is the beginning of the goal-setting process and gives you the chance to make a difference in your life. By writing down what you want to achieve and why, you are allowing your creativity to kick in and free your mind. By writing a weekly action plan and including a timeline to show where you will be in three months, six months and a year from now, you are beginning to write the rest of your life.

Having a system of reviewing, renewing and rewriting – and rewarding yourself regularly – makes it easier to stay on track and to be open and alert to new directions and ideas that come along.

Once we free our minds of self-limiting beliefs and start to document how we feel, what we want and why, the process of change can be amazing and swift. It is important, as part of the writing process, to acknowl-edge all the progress we have made and to celebrate every achievement. It's all too easy to overlook small steps when we are focused on our main goals, but by writing them down in detail we always have a record of our achievements to look back on, keeping us moti-vated to move forward.

Your journal can be the definitive written record of your progress and a constant reminder of how far you have already come. Seeing your achievements in writ-ing promotes positivity and instils excitement, hope and happiness. Writing itself is an activity that devel-ops a great sense of achievement and pride – as well as giving ownership, which is crucial to being fully in control of your new life.

An important element of any personal development and goal-setting work is to carry out regular 'future self' exercises. These are sometimes met with resis-tance by those who struggle to imagine how they will feel when they reach their goals. But through this exercise, people give themselves time to explore what is possible and be really honest about what they want.

WRITE

- Write about what your life will be like when you have achieved your goals. Future self exercises require creative visualisation; writing can play an important part in this process. Writing like this needs to contain a lot of details.

By writing about what we have already achieved and all the steps that we took to get there, we felt an enhanced sense of achievement. This should have made us feel engaged, energised and inspired – full of hope and excitement for the future.

This exercise shouldn't be an endurance test or an arduous, stressful experience that leaves us feeling drained and under pressure. It should fill you with positivity.

Write down your goals and how you will feel when you achieve them. Allowing yourself to dream big is important. Get focused by using the information you have already started to collect in your journal.

This exercise is not a lesson in competitive writing. It is crucial that you are not overly critical of what you write. It's far more important to be honest with yourself about what you want, what makes you happy and what you have done and will do to achieve it.

Writing in all its forms provides us all with a creative way to document our thoughts, feelings, fears, hopes and dreams and to plan goals for our future. We can keep our writing secret or share with others – but the more we integrate writing into our daily routine, the bigger the rewards we can reap. We truly can write the rest of our lives – on our terms and in our notebooks.

The five Cs

- Create

- Curate

- Contribute

- Consider

- Community

Talking about what we would love our lives to look like is great. It's fun – like fantasising about a lottery win – and it forms the basis of many a great night out. But it's much better to actually commit these ideas to paper.

WRITE

In your journal, write down the answers to these questions:

- How can I curate all that is good and all that I need in my life to move forward?

- What do I want my contribution to be?

- How do I want to be considered by my friends and family?

- What does community mean to me?

    - It's important not to edit your answers; just write down as many ideas as you can think of without worrying if they are possible or realistic.

    - Notice how you feel. Excited? Nervous? Maybe a tiny bit scared? Great. That's when you know you are on to something really good.

Tips to make the most of your writing time

Choose what you love

Choose your journals and pens carefully. If you were buying a new laptop, you would spend time checking out the best options; apply the same method to choosing your handwriting equipment. Choose stuff that you love to use – and take good care of it. It has the power to transform your life!

Black and blue?

We often associate blue or black ink with school or work – things that perhaps don't hold great memories for all of us! Choose another colour for writing in your journal. One of my friends uses a rich, indulgent chocolate brown ink for handwriting and another writes in a vibrant, verdant green. I love getting postcards from them!

Dream in detail

Like an artist creating a painting, use writing as your art form and design the life that you desire and deserve. Add detail, colour and inspiration for every single part of the life that you want to lead. Imagine you are living that life right now.

- Make sure you love your journal and pen – choose a pen that is comfortable to hold and a joy to use.

- You don't need to write in perfect prose! Use different colours and styles of writing. Include drawings, scribbles, doodles and diagrams.

- Lists are a really quick and effective way to map out ideas and help you to structure your plans – and they only take a few minutes.

- A mind map drawn in the centre of the page can help you to make connections, see possibilities and discover new ideas.

- Start a vision board. Collect inspiring materials that are relevant to your goals and get creative by curating and arranging them. It provides instant gratification and a constant reminder of your fantastic plans for the future!

CASE STUDY

Having the confidence to make decisions and plans for the future is not always easy. For Ellen, a single mum with two very young children, it was even harder as she had tough life challenges to deal with first.

'Journalling has helped me to realise my dream and make initial steps to start planning again. I now have the courage to believe in myself and stand up for what I want from life. By writing every day, I have really got my confidence back.'

Ellen, single mum of two. Back in control. Future wedding planning expert.

Summary

- You have asked yourself some deep and meaningful questions and started to understand yourself better

- You are already starting to see and feel the impact of daily writing

- You have started to feel more confident about making plans for the future

PART 2

LIFE

Good old life. It's great, isn't it, when everything is falling beautifully into place without any dramas or problems? If only life were always that easy!

In this part of the book you will start to look in detail at your life and unpack it, so that you are clear about what is working and what isn't serving you well. You may not have noticed those things, or have decided to ignore them; we all do it. We will examine the eight-step LIFE EDIT process in more detail and you will learn to understand what's important to you and how to stop fear getting in the way of being fabulous.

The eight-step LIFE EDIT formula for success

The writing exercises that I have developed make us question and investigate all areas of our lives. The process follows a clear eight-step formula for positive change.

The LIFE EDIT formula stands for:

- Let Go, Love your life now and get Limitless!

- Inspire yourself with Ideas. Investigate change.

- Focus on what you really want. Face your Fear. Look to your Future.

- Edit what is not serving you well out of your life. Explore opportunities. Evaluate your progress.

- Empower yourself. Embrace change.

- Define your goals. Decide the way forward.

- Intentions and Integrity are Important.

- Time to Transform!

At the end of each chapter you will find an example of how that part of the eight-step process can help you move forward with different areas of your life.

6
Let Go, Love Your Life Now and Get Limitless!

In this chapter we will learn why it is so important to let go of anything that is stopping you from making positive changes, and to love your life now. This isn't always easy, of course – especially when we are working through challenges. And as for limits – there are no limits to what you can achieve. Never limit your challenges, but always challenge your limits.

By working and writing through the LIFE EDIT's eight stages, we can establish where we are and the editing that we need to do. We can start to plan for the future by writing down what it is we want to achieve, why – and when.

Removing self-limiting beliefs from our minds can be hard but it's so important for success. This is not about arrogance or being a diva; it's about having a robust powerhouse of a self-belief system that supports us through the next chapters of our lives. Clearing all areas of our lives will help us tap into what we really want and how we will get there. And remember, a belief is just that: we can choose to believe it or ignore it. If you are approaching midlife believing that people of your age can't make changes, then it's definitely time to think again.

A daily writing practice is a proven way to get clarity around anything that is not serving you well. By now you know that the simplest way to maintain your new writing ritual is to write down how you feel about one or more areas of your life. Release your worries onto paper and see how much better you feel afterwards. Whether you lack confidence, are worried about your work life or need to sort out health issues, this step will help you let go of any unhelpful beliefs so that you can race into midlife with abundant energy and a new-found lust for life.

By inspecting and investigating different areas of our lives, we can start the editing process and allow our creativity to start working. It gives us a clear view and the time to consider what is really important to us.

Our lives contain a lot of different elements or values. They all have positives and negatives, triumphs and challenges – and they make us who we are. Overcoming challenges may be hard, but it makes us robust and helps us to develop life management strategies.

Here are a few life values to get you started:

- Home
- Family
- Relationships/love/sex
- Friends
- Work
- Volunteering/charity work
- Wealth/finances
- Health and wellbeing
- Spiritualism
- Religious beliefs
- Hobbies and interests
- Information, technology and digital connectivity

All of those different categories make up our lives. Some are more important to us than others, but there are bits of all of them that fit together in all our lives and make up our existence here on this planet.

It's a lot to think about. And while much of the activity associated with each category is (I hope) positive and moving in the right direction, other activities might need a bit of a tweak, a major shift or to have elements deleted altogether. Make sure you take time to look at all of your life; appreciate all the good stuff that is going on as well as anything you need to change.

Life is hectic. We spend much of our time rushing between different responsibilities – family life, jobs, caring for others – and rarely have time to press the pause button on our own life and carry out our own health check. The LIFE EDIT helps you check all the areas of your life, define some goals for midlife marvellousness and enable you to reach them by creating a road map of how to get there. It is crucial that the road map helps you to reach your goal effectively; indeed, without a map or a plan, none of us will get anywhere. Imagine getting in a car and driving without a destination in mind – it would be a pretty pointless exercise.

Imagine trying to reach a goal and make plans while your life is in chaos. You might make some initial progress as your activity will be fuelled by enthusiasm and adrenaline – change can be exciting as well as a great distraction from reality. But without letting go and carrying out an effective editing or clearing process, you will soon hit a bump in the road that will throw you off course and stop you reaching your goal. If we don't first face the facts about how our life is now, no amount of denial or distraction will serve us in our endeavours.

Having a clear pathway is crucial to moving forward and making new plans for the future. Having robust self-esteem and actively letting go of self-limiting beliefs around any areas of your life will serve you well. A daily writing session will support this.

As we know, clutter is no good if we want to make progress. To move forward, we need to let go of anything (and anyone) that is blocking our way. One of the biggest blocks to progress is a lack of self-belief. Like everything else that needs decluttering, it will only hold us back if we don't address it. Many of us harbour long-held beliefs that we are under-achievers in certain areas of our lives.

WRITE

- In your journal, list all the reasons why you believe you cannot achieve something. Why do you believe it? What evidence do you have that supports the claim?

- Then write down all the reasons why you *can* achieve your goals. Remember a belief is just that. We can choose to believe it or not.

- Now write down everything you can think of that makes you:

  - Happy

  - Sad

  - Proud

  - Angry

  - Scared

  - Contented

  - Excited

- Take your time with this exercise and notice your thoughts and feelings as you answer the questions. Work through both the exercises and then read it back – what does your writing tell you about yourself?

Loving your life now

As we make changes and race towards our new goals, it's easy to forget to appreciate what we do have that is already pretty good. I guarantee there are lots of things in your life that fall into this category. You just haven't noticed them yet – or you've got so used to them that you take them for granted. It happens to us all.

When life seems to be working out well for others and not for us, we tend to focus more on negativity, scarcity and lack than on positivity and abundance. This is a perfectly natural reaction. It's hard not to think that the entire world has it in for you when you're trying hard to make changes but getting nowhere fast! This is a particularly salient point for midlifers. Beware of envy – it really is the thief of joy.

To move through this negativity, we need to retrain ourselves to focus more on what is good in our life. We need to consider what we already have and – most importantly – what we have achieved in our lives to this point. Those achievements give us wisdom and experience we can offer both to ourselves and to others.

I am not suggesting we should ignore any challenges we face – in fact, I would urge you to do quite the opposite. Accepting where we are in our lives right now is crucial to working out where we go next and what we will need to do to get there. If some things are not going well, it is essential to identify those things and work through them. This is why daily writing is so important. It allows us to pause rather than panic and to get a clear view of everything that is going on.

A lot of the research regarding gratitude and journalling or writing has been performed by two psychologists, Dr Robert A Emmons of the University of California and Dr Michael E McCullough of the University of Miami. In one study over ten weeks, three groups of students were asked to focus on specific topics each week and write about them.

While one group wrote about everything they were truly grateful for, the other group wrote about things that didn't make them happy, and the third wrote things that had happened to them, but not in a negative or positive way.

It was found that those who wrote a daily gratitude exercise were more optimistic and felt better about their lives. They were also more likely to exercise and had fewer ailments and less visits to their doctor.[7]

---

7   Dr Robert A Emmons of the University of California and Dr Michael
    E McCullough of the University of Miami carried out research into
    gratitude with the study Counting Blessings V Burdens: https://
    greatergood.berkeley.edu/images/application_uploads/Emmons-
    CountingBlessings.pdf

Further research into the impact of writing about positivity was carried out by Dr Martin E P Seligman, a psychologist at the University of Pennsylvania. As part of his study more than 400 people wrote and personally delivered a letter of gratitude to someone who had never been properly thanked for their kindness. Happiness levels of the participants increased dramatically, and they continued to feel more positive a month later.[8]

WRITE

Love your life

- What three things are you immediately grateful for? What do they bring to your life and how would things be different if you didn't have them?

Be limitless

- What have you been talking about doing for ages but not done anything about? Why not? What has stopped you? Why are you choosing to be limited in your ambitions?

- Write down in your journal what it is you want to do and why you haven't yet done it. What do you actively need to let go of to move forward?

---

8   Dr Martin E P Seligman, a psychologist at the University of Pennsylvania and founder of positive psychology, tested the impact of various positive psychology interventions on 411 people: https://greatergood.berkeley.edu/images/application_uploads/Seligman-PosPsychProgress.pdf

We all talk about our ideas and plans for the future – often repeatedly and in great detail – but few of us actually take the time to record those plans on paper. Surely if the ideas are good enough to warrant many hours of conversation, they must be valuable enough to commit to paper?

So why do some people choose not to write down their goals? Is it because they know that if you write something down it all becomes scary and real very quickly? Of course it is. Why don't we listen to ourselves properly? Instead of being limited by challenges, actively challenge your limits. You will be amazed what happens.

Writing is not for everyone; I accept that. There are good reasons why we don't all love writing. It's often because we had negative experiences at school. But journalling or writing every day for self-development as an adult is different from doing our English homework.

CASE STUDY

Michelle improved her literacy by taking adult education classes and then took up daily writing sessions.

'Daily writing really helped me to see the bigger picture and what I could do with my life. I now feel that I will be able to be the best possible version of myself that I can. I will succeed and reach all my goals.'

Michelle, mum. Future F1 mechanic. Inspirational.

Let go of the idea that you have to stay in a job that makes you miserable, doing work that you don't love. Lose the belief that you can't make a career change in midlife. Love the fact that you have amazing skills and experience that you can use differently, to work for yourself or someone else in a role that will make you happy and that could make a difference to others. Love that you are in your prime and you have space to embrace change. Be limitless!

Here's an example of how letting go, loving your life and being limitless can help with your career or job situation.

CASE STUDY

Making big career changes can be frightening and leave you feeling out of your depth. You may feel obligated to keep on doing what you have always done. This was especially true for Jo, who always thought she would follow the same career path.

'I was excited as the opportunity for change was standing right in front of me, but at the same time, I felt quite scared as I had never tried anything like this before. What if I failed? I wanted to change my career. I had studied hard at uni and started on a career path that I thought would last me a lifetime until one day, after twelve years in the industry, I realised I just wasn't happy. I felt unable to pin down what I really wanted to do instead. The writing sessions really helped me to declutter my thoughts and feelings and to focus on what it was that I could be seeking in a career. I was able to understand the thoughts that might be influencing my behaviour, to make sense of all my ideas for a new potential career and then take planned, manageable, realistic steps towards change.'

Jo, former forensic scientist. Emerging voiceover artist. Pocket rocket.

Summary

- You have learned how daily writing helps you to let go of limiting beliefs

- You understand the importance of loving your life now

- You know that you can be limitless in what you choose to achieve

- You have now really started the LIFE EDIT process

7
Inspiration and Ideas

In this chapter, we will look at the importance of making time to develop our ideas and how we can be really inspired to make change.

WRITE

- In your journal, write down the top five areas of your life that cause you the most challenges. Then look at each area in detail. Write down where the problems are and what you think is causing them.

- For example, perhaps you feel a strong loyalty to a friend but they only contact you when they want something? This is a great opportunity to write down how that makes you feel. What can inspire you to make changes? What ideas do you already have to change the situation?

- Perhaps you long for a tranquil garden or changes to your home? Maybe your finances could be in better shape? How can you make improvements that will help with your plans for inspirational changes?

- When you have worked out where the challenges are, write down how you could change things to give you the outcome you desire.

Remember that your journal is personal to you. You never have to share your writing with anyone unless you choose to, but the simple act of letting go of your feelings and seeing them on the page will help you to deal with challenges that have the potential to sabotage even the best-laid plans. Write away the stress of any area of your life and you will soon feel clearer, lighter and better able to cope. You will allow yourself to be inspired to make changes.

Moving forward with a list of exciting and ambitious ideas and plans is a great place to find yourself in. We all want to make changes for a whole host of reasons and planning for exciting times is always good. But it's important to understand why we want to make these changes in the first place, and what the impact will be on the way we live our lives. Writing down not only the plans you are creating and working towards but also your vision for the effect those goals will have is a really important part of the process. It will ensure you are a finisher, not just a starter.

By writing down in great detail our dreams, desires and ideas for the future, we can create a strong visualisation of what our lives will look like when we get there and be inspired to change.

So many of us have great ideas and grand plans – but how many actually come to fruition? Very few. How many of us have been guilty of getting massively excited about a new project or idea, only to run out of steam? Almost all.

Here is a simple way to make sure your daily writing practice really supports your plans for the future.

WRITE

Write down your goals and describe in detail how you will feel and how your life will change when you get there:

- Why is this goal important to you?

- How will it change your life?

- What is inspiring you to make these changes?

- Then write down all the steps that you need to take to get you there. These may change as you work through the process, but by planning ahead, visualising success and describing on paper the impact of these changes, you will strengthen your resolve to keep moving forward. You are less likely to succumb to distraction, your inner critic or the 'fact' that you are just too busy to make any changes.

A quick note about... busyness syndrome

The writing exercises that I have created were designed to fit into a daily schedule and bring instant relief and clarity. The results are pretty good so far!

'Competitive busyness' is one life area that I think writing can help with. I have a long-held theory about busyness and remain convinced that working smarter, not harder is the way to true happiness. It certainly is for me.

I was once out for Saturday night dinner with a group of friends. One arrived very late, citing work. This was not unusual; she is one of those people who always works harder and longer hours than the rest of us. She also left early because she had to work on the Sunday morning.

This particular friend is always 'fried', always rushing and always spinning plates – yet she never seems to get any further forward. She always looks exhausted and stressed.

My theory is this. This friend – along with countless other women I have known over the years – uses tiredness and busyness as badges of honour. There is no doubt that some people have no choice but to work punishingly long hours and there is no getting away from that, but many people create busyness and exhaustion to give the impression they are hugely successful when the reality is quite the opposite. Usually they are swimming upstream, barely keeping their heads above water and worrying far too much about what everyone else is doing. And it's mostly unnecessary.

It's time for all this nonsense to stop. It makes me sad that brilliant women are wearing themselves out. When they come to me for coaching, it's all too apparent that their endless addiction to being manic is not serving them well at all. So many of them say they feel they have to compete. Really?

Being busy can become competitive and addictive and it's easy to use it as a tool for procrastination, avoidance and denial. A good way forward is to pause and take a look at what is really going on by journalling our thoughts. If we revisit our values and priorities, we can reframe our lives and focus on what we need to do – not what we think we need to do. Usually a lot of what we perceive as vital daily activities aren't that vital at all – we've just convinced ourselves that we must be seen to be doing them.

Being endlessly busy doesn't necessarily equate to increased productivity or more success, popularity or wealth – in fact, it just makes us tired and unmotivated.

By writing down our desirable outcomes and focusing on the end result, we soon realise that most of what we fill our days with is superfluous stuff – nothing more than an avoidance tactic. By stripping this away, we can quickly make actual progress.

If we take time every day to write in our journals, we can nip this kind of thing in the bud. We give ourselves valuable headspace to re-evaluate every day if we need to. We make sure we are using our time and energy to move towards actions that will, ultimately, give us fulfilment, happiness and a desirable outcome.

We are often so busy racing to achieve and be the best, the richest or the most successful that we fill our days with 'must-do' actions that are actually pretty meaningless. It's time to stop being busy for busy's sake and refocus our efforts on making proper progress that will give us what we really want, not what we think we should have just because everyone else has it.

Daily writing gives us a chance to reflect on what we have already achieved. We remind ourselves how far we have come and how grateful we are for all that we already have in our lives. It's easy to overlook all this when we are racing around. Even when we do arrive at our goals, we're often too exhausted to enjoy them or to acknowledge what we achieved along the way.

Daily writing in a journal is the way to make a powerful and inspirational start towards your goals. It will give you clarity, inner confidence, drive and motivation. Grab that pen and start making the magic happen.

WRITE

Every week, write the answers to these questions in your journal:

- What is my main goal?

- Why is it important? What will it mean to me when I have achieved it?

- What steps can I take during the next five days to move closer to this goal?

- How will I do this?

- What help or support will I need?

- When I have completed these steps, how will I reward myself?

- What has happened in the last week to make me happy, sad, angry or worried?

- What were my three big wins in the last week?

- Have I been consciously using my daily writing to help me work towards my goals?

- What have I learned so far?

- What am I most grateful for right now?

CASE STUDY

All forms of creativity can help to give us space and time to pause, focus and consider our options.

For Hayley, reframing past experiences by asking herself important questions was just the beginning.

'I have loved my writing sessions and they have helped to change my life in just a few weeks. I now have the tools to carry on improving my life for the future. I really enjoyed creating my inspiration board and now have self-improvement tools that I will carry with me for the rest of my life.'

Hayley, recovering from addictions. Mum. Happy. Inspirational. Game changer.

An example of how inspiration can help how you feel about yourself.

Get inspired to change your look: your clothes, hair and make-up, even your perfume. Get together with trusted friends and have a clothes swap, makeover party or shopping trip. You can all have a fashion update at the same time. Be inspired by the style of someone you admire – but use your own ideas to see how a new look could make you feel better and put you back in control. If you look good, you will feel good. That will give you the confidence to move forward with grace, courage and integrity.

Summary

- We looked at the need to get inspired in each area of our lives so that we can grow our ideas for change

- We now know that we can be inspired to make change by documenting what is working well and what isn't

8
Focus, Fear and Your Future

In this chapter, we will look at the importance of staying focused and how fear of midlife should never be allowed to get in the way of creating your new future.

This is an exciting, creative and life-changing journey. By now, you should be thinking seriously about how you would like your midlife to be and what you can do to make things happen. You should have focus.

It's always a brave move to confront parts of our lives that are not working well, but writing it all down in daily bite-sized chunks makes it much easier. It stops the fear gripping you.

Fear of failure is a big stumbling block for many people. As soon as we commit to writing our ideas down there is a record, there in black and white. The action of transferring messages from our heads and our hearts to a notebook is powerful and that is why the LIFE EDIT works so effectively. This is especially true in midlife – a time when we can easily start to feel foolish. We may be frightened by the prospect of change, but equally frightened by the idea of no change at all.

When I was a child and a teenager, I kept a diary. I documented everything I was worried about and all the things I feared. I wrote stuff about good-looking boys (didn't we all) – but also about what I wanted to do with my life. I wrote about things that happened to my friends because I wished they would happen to me; I was modelling myself on them. That is something I'm pleased to say I have learned not to do as a midlife adult.

Some of the things I documented came true. I never got any good at woodwork or metalwork classes – but I was lucky enough to own a horse and I did become a journalist. Eventually I found a boyfriend, too. And, thankfully, some of those thoughts have stayed where they belong – as teenage fantasies in a different time and place.

There is something incredibly powerful and impactful about the act and art of writing that enables us to achieve the things we decide to commit to paper.

Journalling or keeping a diary are not new, but the way we can use it to focus on thoughts and ideas and make them work for us in a positive way can give us tremendous strength and help us to lead a fulfilled and purposeful life.

In this digital age of super-fast information and the huge range of platforms where we can document every moment of our lives, it is easy to overlook the power of the traditional pen and paper. As a journalist and a writer, I positively embrace all platforms and methods of communication. I would not have stayed gainfully employed had I not become tech-savvy, but as a personal development coach I truly believe that handwriting works. It works for me and for lots of the people I've worked with. It can work for you, too.

When I work with people, I look at how things are in their lives now and then help them to move forward, using writing as a way of editing, curating, goal-setting and planning – and leading ultimately to a new life.

I developed the LIFE EDIT to help people pause, edit the noise from their lives and minds and create goals that will lead to a more fulfilled and positive life. I am not ignoring or denying the fact that we all have difficult times to deal with. But I have seen for myself that the change and improvements in people's lives when they start to write down their goals in a journal are immense; I invite you to embrace this method and look forward to positive changes.

Having a clear sense of purpose and focus to our lives is vital. We need to remind ourselves regularly of our goals and find ways to keep moving forward. Writing can help to reframe the way we feel about negative events and provide us with essential hope, optimism and purpose. It helps us reframe, regain focus and deal with fear while we keep looking towards the future.

A daily writing practice is a proven way to find clarity around anything that is not helping your life right now. The simplest way to start your new ritual is to write down how you feel about one or more areas of your life. Release your worries onto paper, and see how much better you feel afterwards.

CASE STUDY

If you already enjoy writing, extending that interest into a daily journalling activity to promote positive change should be relatively easy.

For Natalie, a keen creative writer and poet, this was definitely the case.

'This was one of the best decisions I have ever made in my life. I went from being a stay-at-home mum, too anxious to even think about doing anything else, to applying for jobs within a matter of weeks.'

Natalie, addicted to learning. Qualified as a teaching assistant. Excellent life juggler.

An example of how focus, fear and your future can help with decisions about your home.

Focus on what isn't working in your home or garden and think about how you could change it to work better. Why do you want to change it? Focus on what the outcome will be and how you will feel when it is completed. Write down what you fear about making the changes – and then think about what your future will look like if you give in to fear and don't make them.

Summary

- Having a clear pathway is crucial to moving forward and making new plans for the future

- Having robust self-esteem and getting rid of self-limiting beliefs will serve you well

- A daily writing session will support this process

9
Edit. Explore. Evaluate.

The dictionary definition of the word 'edit' is: 'To prepare (written material) for publication by correcting, condensing or otherwise modifying it.'

You can apply this to your life. Prepare the rest of your life by correcting, condensing or otherwise modifying it.

By now we all know that the first stage towards reaching those all-important goals is to create clarity in every area of your life. Write down everything that is really, truly bothering you – then make a plan to tackle it all. Keeping a written record of progress and an action plan or to-do list will make the process even more satisfying.

For the purposes of this process and to put you in a positive space to achieve your goals, we will look at every aspect of your life in detail. We will list all that is good, all that is not so good, and what you would like it to look like in the future.

Unless you go through the LIFE EDIT process to clear your life physically, mentally and emotionally, you will find moving towards your goals really difficult – and you will inevitably be inclined to give up.

This is why editing, exploring and evaluating are such a vital part of this process. Effective editing now will ensure that you build your future self on solid foundations. An effective way to think of this is as a building. It doesn't matter how neat the brickwork is, or how expensive the building materials are – without sound foundations, your building will not stay upright for long.

By detailing the problem areas, you will find a solution to sorting them out. You will also create a permanent record to show your problem-solving skills – and how far you have come.

WRITE

- By now you will be looking at the different areas of your life regularly. Write a list of everything you think you need to clear immediately. Don't think too much – just write down, fast, the first things that come into your head. When you have finished, look at the list (or lists) you have made. Edit them to create a top ten of things that need to be sorted. This exercise will help you to focus properly on what you need to tackle.

Glossing over problems, dilemmas or other little niggles – no matter how small they may seem – will not help you to move forward. You may get a little way along your life-planning journey, but your plan will start to flounder. Without effective and honest editing, you will hit a bump in the road and may find it difficult to get back on track.

If this happens, simply go back to basics and clear that problem before moving on. Write about what happened, why, and how it made you feel.

WRITE

- Sometimes writing a letter, to either yourself or the situation or person that caused the challenge, can really help. You don't have to send it; just writing about how the situation has made you feel will make you feel much better. I do it often. Funnily enough, I'm a normal person with normal challenges!

- Try this now and see how much clearer and lighter you feel afterwards. It may also give you ideas for how to manage other challenges.

Failure is only feedback

Remember that if things don't work out, this is simply feedback. Document what happened, and I guarantee that once the ink starts flowing, you will find your solution right there on the page. Don't overthink it – just let the words dance across the page to bring you the clarity you need.

Many of us have niggling little problems and issues in our lives. They run in the background like annoying computer programs that use too much memory and slow your laptop down. Every now and then, a notification pops up, telling us we must take some sort of action, but we hit the snooze button and move on with our day. And then our laptop crashes, causing us major stress.

Editing is a vital part of this process. Problems may appear small and insignificant, but they all need to be dealt with appropriately. As we embrace midlife, it's likely that we have successfully avoided or ignored lots of small problems. They may have become normal and accepted parts of our lives. But we ignore them at our peril.

Niggling problems – physical, environmental or emotional – all rent space in our head and sap our energy. We can only ignore them for so long before they put blockages in our way. And that is why editing is crucial. Until you clear these problems, you will never know how they were holding you back.

The energy you free up will allow you to make amazing and positive changes in your life, will clear your mind and help you even more with your daily writing exercises.

This will help to set you firmly on the path to success, as well as being really satisfying. For many of us, clearing our lives can be an emotional process. This is normal, so don't be floored by how you feel. It's time to let go and deal with anything stopping you from having the positive life and success that you deserve.

With all this in mind, it's time to start your life edit properly and get some clarity around the next stage of your life.

WRITE

- Spend some time thinking about and writing down any areas of your life that you need to edit. This is not about being spoilt, selfish or demanding. It is about making you the best you can be and facing midlife head-on. Spending time fathoming out what to do next and how to do it will benefit both you and the other people in your life.

When you are editing, there may be particular areas you wish to concentrate on. Here are some of them.

Your home

This can be overwhelming for many people, so break it down to a single room. If you need to, reduce it even further by focusing on a particular cupboard, drawer or box. This is particularly challenging for empty-nesters coping with their children leaving home. They often want to hang on to stuff because they find it hard that their children have moved on to the next phase of their lives. My advice would be this: let them go. Adjust in your own time. Launching into a massive clear-out the day after you dispatched them to their new abode won't necessarily help. Some people describe this period of their life as a type of bereavement – so take it one step at a time.

Write a list of what you need to do, why, and what the outcome will be. For example:

- Action: Clear my wardrobe. Take clothes to charity shop/recycle/give to friends.
- Why: A tidy space ready to update my look.
- Result: A fresh new confident me.

Always focus on the expected outcome when you write. That way you will stay focused and motivated.

Success with this kind of life editing is a matter of scale and managing expectations. If your entire home needs clearing, this can be emotionally challenging and overwhelming. Don't be too hard on yourself; take small steps towards clarity. That way, the process remains manageable, achievable and ultimately satisfying. It stays within your control.

Even if you only clear one shelf a week, that's a huge step forward. Set it as your goal for the week and celebrate when you achieve it. We are often not very good at celebrating small steps towards our goals; our focus is always on the final big goal. But the smaller goals we meet along the way are crucial to achieving our overall success. We should celebrate all of them.

Hoarding and living surrounded by stuff can indicate a much wider challenge that requires specialist help and support. I can't cover that here, but there are lots of people who can help you. If you're feeling overwhelmed and stuck, seek advice from your friends, family, community or healthcare professionals before embarking on the LIFE EDIT programme.

Your car and your work luggage

If your car can best be described as a skip on wheels, then now is the time for a big, serious clear-out! We don't all love our cars, but the way you take care of yours says a great deal about your mindset. You don't even have to do it yourself; if you prefer, pay someone to do it for you.

Make a list such as:

- Clear out all the rubbish.

- Give the car a good clean inside and out so that it smells great and shines.

- Do a bit of basic running maintenance.

- Put in a new air freshener or some fresh screen wash.

Apply a similar approach to your luggage. Our work bags and handbags speak volumes. It's all too easy to cram them full of stuff that we end up carrying around with us forever. So clear out all the junk and refill your bag with the things you need and want to carry around. You will be carrying a lighter load in more ways than one. For this process to work, it helps to have a clear vision of what you really hope to achieve. You also need to start being more organised about life in general, but a clear mind is completely achievable by taking these small steps now.

Write a list of everything you really need to carry with you and only put those items back in your bag. Don't forget to include a notebook and pen!

Relationships

Only you can decide if your relationships are holding you back. Our partners, friends and families are important parts of our lives; if they are good friends, they will support you in your endeavours. If you find them criticising you and finding fault then you may have to make some difficult decisions around how to move forward. The most important part of this entire process is you. You are the priority.

Spend time writing about the important people in your life. Write letters to them explaining where you are in your life and what your plans are. Ask for their support or encouragement and suggest ways they can help you.

Emotional editing

Nobody is perfect. We've all made mistakes. But it's important to forgive yourself and others – this is the only way to move forward successfully. Holding on to regrets or difficult past challenges will never release you from any shame, fear or blockages that are holding you back. It is time to forgive and move on.

Physical and lifestyle

This part of the editing process enables you to take a good, detailed look at your lifestyle, diet and general health. It's not about being critical or judgemental, but it is about looking at health and diet niggles that could be holding you back.

Look at your current diet, lifestyle, exercise regime and any health niggles – no matter how minor – and make a list of any areas that you feel could benefit from some changes.

Changing old habits is hard. But it's a pivotal part of the positive life-planning process as it lets us put techniques in place to stop us derailing our plans.

Niggling problems can fester, especially if left untreated. The way you treat your own body symbolises the way you treat yourself and what you think you're worthy of in terms of changing your outlook, setting new goals and achieving them.

Identify any physical niggles you may have. Be kind to yourself and start investing in your most valuable asset: you.

How I edited part of my own life

My own story is a good example of the reality of clearing. The process can cause turmoil and exhaustion – but there is a happy ending.

Having lived as a single parent for thirteen years, by the time my fabulous husband came along I had pretty much given up the idea of ever being part of a couple again. After 100 – yes, 100! – disastrous internet dates I had hung up my dating shoes for good and accepted singledom as my calling. In fact, I had inadvertently set a goal to find a man who loved me 'just the way I am' (thanks, Bridget Jones!). I didn't realise it was a goal at the time but now I know the universe had other ideas.

My house, my head and my friendships all screamed 'hoarder!' and the idea of starting a new relationship was pretty much a headf**k. The house was cluttered; I hadn't been able to remove signs of my children's baby or toddler years. I had one friendship in particular that I thought was great but was actually a disaster. My whole life was holding me back.

I was broke, exhausted, struggling and putting on a great act that everything was fine and dandy. I know now that FINE stands for:

- F****d Up
- Insecure
- Neurotic
- Exhausted

I really was FINE!

Slowly but surely, though, my fantastic new man helped me audit and edit every area of my life. I had no idea how bad things had become. He encouraged and helped me to get rid of stuff, including the children's toys. When I asked the kids if they wanted to keep them, do you know what they said? 'To be honest, Mum, we thought you got rid of all that stuff years ago! Why on earth have you kept it?'

I'd kept it because I was scared. Letting go of anything is hard. It's an emotional wrench having to make decisions about possessions and people that have been in your life for a long time. Sometimes you need the fresh eyes of someone who loves and cares about you to stand back and see the whole picture. They can help you to move forward because they can see your potential. You can't, because your head, heart and home are full of stuff.

The revamp of our sad, decaying garden started with the removal of an ugly concrete post and the burning of a dilapidated shed; I went out for an hour and came back to a bonfire. It is now an oasis and I have a beautiful studio surrounded by lush plants and trees.

The edit of our home started when my previous office, a cupboard under the stairs, was requisitioned as a shower room. We now have a truly beautiful home.

And the edit of my friendships started once I had the clarity and space to see how badly I had been treated by the one person I thought would be my friend forever.

Yes, it was hard. But the rewards were immense. Life just gets better and better – so trust me on this one. Audit, edit, write, repeat.

Honesty is the best policy. If you are clear about what you want, the parts of your life that need attention will soon become clear. The simplest, smallest edits can often make the biggest difference, and a robust life audit will indicate where changes need to be made. Be kind to yourself and take your time. Editing is a painstaking process which is all in the detail. Embrace the process – it isn't designed to make you feel weak or like a failure! You cannot make plans and live a positive existence if there are underlying problems that need attention.

Make sure that you write down every single detail of what needs to be cleared and how you feel about it. It's OK to be sad or anxious, but you must also document how you feel during and after the clearing process – and remember to celebrate your achievements. Sometimes a simple change like switching up your hairstyle or taking a twenty-minute walk every day can have a huge impact on how you feel about yourself.

Morning Pages and Evening Reflection

By incorporating these two specific writing exercises into your daily routine now, you will start to see transformations taking place.

WRITE

Morning Pages

- This writing exercise is also called 'free writing' and is simply that. Allow yourself ten to fifteen minutes each morning to write freely about anything at all. Doing this will give you clarity for the day ahead and a chance to edit anything from your life that you need to be rid of.

Evening Reflection

- Every evening, spend fifteen minutes reflecting and thinking about what has happened during the day. Recall how you dealt with certain situations and how you felt. This is a great way to overcome challenges and obstacles and to acknowledge and celebrate your wins. However small they may be, they are important. We spend too much time rushing to the finish line, rarely stopping to think about how far we have come. It is vital to reward ourselves when we achieve anything – and a reflective writing practice is a great reminder.

Make the most of your writing time

Planning to create exciting changes is a brilliant thing to do. It's a chance to look at what is really going on for us, and then to clear our path and make progress towards our goals.

To lead a purposeful, happy and fulfilled existence, it is vital that the most important areas of our life – like family, home, work, health, wealth, and relationships – are strong and stable. Choose the things that matter most to you.

1. Select one area of your life to investigate.

2. How are you really doing in that area? Be brutally honest with yourself. Write down what is working well for you and what definitely isn't.

3. Now describe what you *want* that area of your life to look like. Include lots of detail.

4. Think about what changes you need to make and what help and support you may need to make them.

5. Repeat for the other areas of your life.

Make room for exciting changes

Editing our lives helps us to remove anything that doesn't work well and replace it with something that does.

We should all take time to edit our lives regularly, but we rarely do; stuff builds up and gets in the way. When we do decide to make a change, we get stuck and disenchanted and then give up. But not any more!

Adopt a regular editing routine and you will see results.

Tips for an energising edit

1. This is a positive step towards change. Be sure to be grateful for all you already have that works well in your life.

2. Editing does not have to mean deleting! Small adjustments and tweaks are sometimes all we need for amazing progress.

3. How is your confidence and self-belief? Be really honest with yourself. Do you believe you can make changes or is something holding you back?

4. How do you want to grow? What do you want to experience and what contribution do you want to make? Write the answers down and use them to guide you as you edit the different areas of your life.

5. Don't get overwhelmed. Take one area at a time and make small, manageable changes. Celebrate each success and harness the positive energy. You can do this.

An example of how editing, exploring and evaluating can help with friendships and relationships:

We all need our team of champions – our cheerleaders, our fans and our friends – especially when we are looking to make changes to our lives. But the edit is a good opportunity to look closely at the people in your life and ask yourself if they really are on your team.

Do you have people (as I did) who you think are on your side but who are actually fair-weather friends, there when the times are good but never when the s**t hits the fan? Editing, exploring and evaluating people in this way seems harsh but it is necessary. This is your time to shine. You need good people around you.

Summary

- We all have things in our life that need editing – from our own belief systems to our wardrobes, our friendships and our job choices

- Getting into the habit of regular editing and deleting or tweaking as necessary will really help you make changes

- Using your daily writing habit is the quickest way to get clarity and clear the fog

PART 3

EDIT

In part three, you will find out about how you can embrace your new confidence and self-belief and be empowered to make inspirational changes. We also look at the importance of defining your goals and making your decisions with integrity. And then it's transformation time.

10

Embrace Empowerment

Excitement and enthusiasm are vital for making positive changes. You need plenty of energy to stay motivated and ensure your momentum doesn't start to slow. Underpinning all of this is empowerment.

Embracing your new-found confidence to make change will propel you forward and keep you on track. It will help you to make clear decisions and take ownership. In this chapter, we will look at all the ways that daily writing can develop your empowerment. You will see how to work out what your strengths are and where challenges and opportunities for change exist. You will identify any threats that might sabotage your progress.

WRITE

- First, write down everything in your life that really matters to you. How do you feel about it? Are you happy with the way things are or do you need to make some changes? Who can you ask for help? Sometimes a new opinion or perspective can empower you to make those all-important changes.

- Do you need extra information, resources or support to help you move forward? Not being empowered to move forward sometimes comes down to lack of knowledge or information as much as lack of self-belief.

- Write an action list of anything that could empower you to embrace change. Break it down into short, snappy sentences or phrases that inspire and promote action. Even if you're not sure what to do next, just write down anything you think could possibly help.

- Use sticky notes to write down actions, words or phrases that will support you in your decision-making. Make energetic notes, fuelled with enthusiasm.

- Make a plan. Schedule in anything you need to act on and specifically aim to get at least two steps closer to your goal each week. Think confidently about simple actions you can take to get closer to making those changes, and you will feel empowered to start making them.

- Finally, answer these questions:

  - What will happen if I don't make a decision?

  - What will happen if I do make a decision?

Empowered writing with focus, care and attention will give you clarity, a framework for the future and the chance to pause, reflect and breathe. You are already seeing that a daily writing practice can make you feel better and more productive after just a few days.

Taking this one step further, making time to be aware of our personality and character traits is a big part of making adjustments and moving forward. Knowing ourselves well instantly empowers us to make changes.

A tried and tested method for doing this is to examine:

• Strengths that we can call on

• Challenges we are facing

• Opportunities that exist to help us

• Fears we may have about making changes

• Interference that may hinder our progress

Take time to look at each of these in turn. Write down as much as you can about each one as it relates to you.

We need to keep in mind that we can work through setbacks and we need to keep our positive mindset in the face of obstacles and unexpected life events. Embracing empowerment will help us to do that. Learning about ourselves and the way we cope and react to different situations gives us the inner strength we need to get past obstacles.

Choosing to adopt a positive mindset – and it is a choice – will help you to keep your focus and stick to your plan in the long run. You will automatically feel empowered to manage situations confidently as they arise.

Over time, we can shift our mindset and patterns of behaviour and reframe past experiences. We can learn to listen carefully to our own thoughts and feelings and then choose how we react to situations.

You cannot base your happiness on something that hasn't happened yet – an increase in wealth or a decrease in dress size. Proclaiming that you will be 'happy when…' is unlikely to help you move forward. But being happy with what you have now, and writing it down regularly, will help you get nearer to your goals; you will reinforce your gratitude and focus more on what is working well. By using your daily writing routine as a structure for your plans, you will feel empowered to keep moving forward.

WRITE

- Write about a particular time or event in your life when things did not go according to plan. Describe what happened and why. Think about your strengths and challenges at that time. Now change the scenario to one that had a positive outcome. Notice how you feel when you use positive rather than negative words – and how empowering it is to change the scenario.

Embracing empowerment: finances and wealth

Money can be scary and it's something that few of us talk about openly. But it is better to be in control of your finances, even if you know you are in the red. Use empowerment to tackle your finances head-on. Stop ignoring the bills. Instead, grip the situation with confidence and be empowered to make a plan. Write lists of actions you need to take to get back on track; be empowered to take them. The clue is in the word. You have the power, so use it – I promise you will feel much better.

A quick note about... fake positivity

I get asked a lot about positivity. I have one 'friend' who simply cannot stand the fact that I am often positive; he maintains the whole thing is complete nonsense and that I am deluded. But I am a regular human being; I am not positive all of the time by any means.

Despite what some people may think, I do not advocate positivity as an avoidance strategy for dealing with all the stuff life throws at us on a regular basis. You cannot have a full life without dealing with sadness, grief, anger, frustration and, yes, negativity. All of these emotions are valuable. They help us deal with life, they give us vital coping strategies and they enable us to navigate life's most treacherous emotional upheavals.

We will all have to cope with challenging times. While I write and teach a lot about finding ways to be positive, the work I do is so much more than that. It's about having the confidence to believe in yourself and trust that you can cope when things start to get difficult, rather than letting your reaction to a situation derail you.

Maintaining a balanced outlook that enables you to draw on positivity can help enormously when the going gets tough, but you cannot ignore the difficult stuff. That has to be dealt with first.

Fake positivity is not a good thing. Genuine positivity is. Even if you have it in spades, you will still encounter difficult times when you simply cannot or do not want to be positive. That's fine. Those times make you who you are and give you the resilience to get through it.

If you have coping mechanisms that you can bring out and use when you need to, that is where positivity truly lies. It is the ability to see past obstacles, to dig deep and find some good, to know that things will eventually get better. I use positivity to help me move forward – but I always acknowledge the situation, accept it and then plan for positive change.

When I was talking to a client about how having an attitude of gratitude is really helpful, she told me a story. She had been a drug addict, a convicted drug dealer, sleeping rough and living a life of danger and chaos. She admitted that finding an ounce of positivity in that situation was hard – but she eventually got to a point where she knew things had to change and she somehow found the energy to make that change. Now she is grateful for things most of us take for granted: a warm bed, a safe place to live, food in the fridge. Being grateful and finding positivity has really helped her, but she did find it hard at times.

You can't be positive all the time and there's no point in faking it. If things aren't going well, you need to declutter, get some clarity and then move forward. That is how adopting a realistic, but more positive, outlook can help you make significant, lasting changes.

Summary

- Embracing empowerment is not about being bossy, domineering or arrogant. It is about having the quiet self-confidence and self-assurance to make the right decisions for you and to build the life that you want to live.

- Empowerment comes from deleting self-limiting beliefs and knowing your worth. It comes from valuing yourself and your plans for the future.

- Be empowered.

11
Delete. Define. Decide.

You should be feeling lighter, clearer and more able to focus and define how you want your life to look as you move forward. In this chapter, we will look at deleting anything else that isn't helping you move forward, defining your goals and deciding how you want your new life to look and feel.

Daily writing is an excellent tool, and you should return to the edit exercises as often as you need to. In time, you will find you are in control of your life rather than letting it overwhelm you. You will have a bulletproof way to deal with anything – which means no more wasted time or procrastination, only progress. Daily writing is the key to getting clarity, defining your goals and deleting anything in your life that will not be able to support you effectively as you move forward.

Many people find themselves unable to ask for what they really want. They end up compromising or procrastinating. Using a daily writing practice, you can be specific, clear and definite about what you want. Only you can decide – and only you have the right to decide – how you live your life. Be specific and definite when you make your plans and you will find the right opportunities will come your way. Anything that doesn't help you can be deleted.

It is a well-known scientific fact that like attracts like, and a mountain of research backs that theory up. Often referred to as the law of attraction, on a scientific level the process involves the RAS and it has been used by life coaches, tutors and authors for years.[9]

The RAS is the portal through which nearly all information enters the brain. It filters this information and governs what you pay attention to, how interested or tuned in you are, and what does not reach the conscious parts of your brain.

Put simply, when we set goals – short, medium or long-term – your brain knows they're important and notices anything that might relate to them. It's important to write down your goals every day so that your

9   www.thelawofattraction.com/what-is-the-law-of-attraction

brain is wired to receive the right information to help you move forward.

To consciously attract the things you choose into your life, you must learn to bring your thoughts and actions into harmony with whatever your goal is – be it perfect health, success, abundance, true love or anything else. Creative visualisation is the basic technique by which you can effectively reprogramme your subconscious mind and attract to yourself the things and circumstances that you have chosen.

Now that you've cleared some space in your life, it's time to dig deeper and set more goals in line with what you really want. It's important to be clear and definite about what you want. Think of your goals like an order.

WRITE

- Spend some time now really thinking about your goals and writing down exactly what you want to achieve. Use mind-mapping to create a map showing what you are aiming for and how you think you will get there. Try to imagine how you will feel when you reach your first goal. What are two things that you could do right now to help you get two steps closer to that goal, however small?

Creative visualisation is used by business people, politicians and sportspeople alike. Far from being some strange, magical ritual, it's an excellent way to create success and positivity. It may seem indulgent – even a bit strange – to allocate time in our busy schedules to imagine what our life could be like if we achieved certain goals, but it's an important part of personal development. As a vital part of your progress, it should not be overlooked.

Visualising success lets us design our ideal life. It's something you should try to integrate into every day so that it becomes a habit. Soon you will be doing this without even realising it; staying positive and moving forward will help you reach your goals. It will help you to upgrade your life by focusing your attention on what you want. That, in turn, will create ways for you to achieve it.

The key to manifesting change is to feel it before you can bring it into existence. Olympic athletes do it all the time; they rehearse their success in advance. You can do it, too, and using daily writing activities is the perfect way to kickstart the process.

A quick note about... indecisiveness

It's not procrastination. It's not laziness or stubbornness. It is simply an inability to make a decision and it can happen for a number of reasons.

We might be motivated to make change but unclear about what steps to take next. We might fear stepping into the unknown, which could be affecting our ability to make clear decisions. Maybe we are avoiding a decision because we can't decide if we're doing the right thing.

Information overload can also easily bring us to a standstill. Not being able to pick out the relevant information from the internal chatter can kill our progress and make a decision appear impossible. The reality is usually that we simply need to sift through the information – edit it, in other words – so that we have only the things we need to help us move forward and define our goals. Reaching a point of overwhelm can scupper even the best-laid plans, causing us to lose valuable time and our focus, but there are simple, quick ways to get back on track and give us the self-belief we need to make those potentially life-changing decisions.

Writing with focus, care and attention gives you clarity, a framework for the future and the chance to pause, reflect and breathe. Do it every day and see how much better you feel and how much more productive you are after just a few days.

There is a good, tried and tested way to make sure that whatever you are aiming for will happen and that you have a definite plan for success.

My version is SMAART:

- Specific
- Meaningful
- Ambitious
- Achievable
- Relevant
- Timed

Make sure that all your goals fit this formula.

By using this acronym for all of your writing and goal-setting, you will be on a firm footing towards change and improvement, whatever you are trying to achieve.

When we make plans, it's easy to get carried away. Planning something new is the most exciting part of the process in so many ways. You're brimming with ideas, enthusiasm and excitement. Your confidence and commitment are back, your energy levels are high; you are dedicated and tuned in to your new idea. Great – but what happens when things don't work out as quickly or effectively as you had hoped? What happens when you hit that bump in the road? For most of us, the answer is easy: we give up and blame our lack of progress on anything we can – usually external forces, rarely ourselves. The reality of the situation is usually that we haven't given enough thought to how we will achieve our aim, or even if it's actually achievable in the first place. We have made assumptions.

Using SMAART will ensure that your plans are robust and you are prepared and resilient.

Is your goal or idea defined and specific?

Have you drilled down and really unpacked the idea? Do you have a definite aim in mind? Have you written down the net result of achieving this particular thing? How will achieving it impact on your life? Why is it so important to you? Have you written down, in detail, the answers to these questions?

Are you fuelled by genuine ambition? Are you working towards something new for the right reasons? Are you clear in your aims for this goal? Is it really achievable?

Dreams are great but unless you can be honest about how to achieve them, they will simply stay as dreams. I'm all for setting audacious goals but if yours seem a little out of reach, tweak them or look again at how you can achieve them – perhaps by taking more time, asking for more information or help, or breaking them down into smaller goals.

Are your plans aligned with your personality? Are they relevant to your skills, your aims and objectives, your available time and resources, and the changes

you want to make? Spend time writing through this
to make sure.

Putting a time limit on anything you're aiming for is
crucial. If you don't have a deadline in mind, things
will drift on and on. Get a diary or a planner and
reverse-engineer your plan; work backwards from
your deadline and write down every single step you
need to take to get there. Write with intent and be specific about the individual steps, the information you
need to find and any research you will need to do.

An example of how you can use the delete, define and
decide step to improve your health and wellbeing:

Making a conscious decision to change how you look
and feel is a pretty loaded choice to make. You must
make sure you're doing it for all the right reasons.
Defining how you want to feel about yourself and
why this is important to you are the first steps in the
process. Perhaps you want to lose some weight to
feel healthier, more comfortable and more energetic?
Maybe you want to shed those feelings of midlife
mediocrity and start living your best life with a body,
mind and wardrobe to match? Perhaps you have a
special occasion coming up and you want to look and
feel amazing? Whatever your reasons, define them
by writing about how the new you will look and
feel. What will you wear? How will your hair and
make-up look? How will you walk and talk? How
will you feel about having your photo taken? Delete

any nagging doubts or negative talk – from either yourself or other people – and write positive words and affirmations to seal the deal you're making with yourself. Decide to win.

Summary

- In this chapter, we have looked at how we can define our goals, decide what we want our life to look like and consider what really needs deleting

- You have made sure that the goals you are working towards fit the SMAART formula

- You have started to work backwards from your deadline to see what you must now do to reach your goal

12
Intentions And Integrity

I t's time to check in with yourself to make sure your intentions for change have integrity and that you are ready to transform. By now, you should have embraced your daily writing habit and be well on the way to your marvellous midlife future. In this final chapter, we will look at lists. You should be setting intentions to succeed with integrity and setting a time limit to reach your goals.

The word 'wish' often gets a bad press. I am not in the business of giving people false hope and I get irritated by people saying things like, 'I wish I could win the lottery – then everything would be OK,' or, 'I wish I could lose weight – then I would be really happy.'

If you wish for change, that's fine to a point – but let's take it one step further. Let's use writing to build an intentional list that goes way beyond a pipe dream and is underpinned by integrity. Wishing is not the same as planning with intent. It is not the same as being proactive and it is not the same as visualising how you want your life to look. Creating a list is all of those things – and I guess one way to look at it would be as a wish list.

Lists are brilliant, deceptively powerful tools that carry a lot of weight and have a huge impact when used properly. You can write lists for just about any-thing: simple weekly to-do lists, lists of your favourite places, books or movies, and lists of things you want to do with your life. Ticking off tasks on a to-do list is one of the most satisfying things you can do. You only have to tick one thing off each day to be winning at life.

Lists are powerful because they are simple. But don't be deceived by their apparent simplicity, because they hold the power to create significant change. How?

Firstly, they are easy and quick. You can dash off a list in no time and there, right in front of you, you have a power-packed, handwritten call to action.

The actions will probably be short sentences, phrases or even single words and they are hard to ignore. We've all had that nagging feeling that we have to tick something off our list – and the feeling when we do it is beyond satisfaction.

Lists are your new best friend! Using lists, we can drill down to create our own pros and cons exercise. We can work things out, we can use bullet points, colours, illustrations, graphs and diagrams. Lists are hard to ignore because they are made with such commitment, and that's why they are an important part of the LIFE EDIT programme. I use them all the time.

Start making lists every day. List your goals, then break those goals down into mini- or micro-goals or steps. Make another list of everything you need to do to achieve just one of those steps. Each day, tick off all the actions you have completed. It will feel great, trust me.

You can start building the list for your life in the same way. List all the things you would like to change, things you need to do to make those changes, and all the ways those changes will make your life better.

Once we choose to adopt a positive mindset, positive things head our way. Our brain continually filters the huge quantity of information in the world around us and lets relevant information through based on the parameters we set. If we act with positive intention, integrity, grace and courage and if we habitually focus on positive things – especially through our daily writing exercises – that will gradually become the 'lens' through which our brain sees the world. Positive affirmations are a great way to project positivity and be intentional in our actions, thoughts and feelings. If we are serious about changing the way we think and feel, we need to choose words that reinforce rather than undermine our positive mindset. There is no such thing as an empty statement; all words carry power.

When we constantly think and talk about ourselves in negative terms – when we tell ourselves, 'I can't' – we invite negativity into our lives. But if we can banish negative thoughts, and instead say intentionally, 'I can,' we shift our mindset and project positive energy.

As part of your writing activity, it's a good idea to spend some time collecting and curating positive, inspiring words that back up your ideas with integrity and intention. These could be your own words, or quotes from others that you have heard or read.

Write them down in your journal every day and display them prominently in your home. Keep a list in your journal of words that inspire and motivate you. If you encounter negative or passive words, replace them with words that resonate much better with you and your plans. As well as writing them down, say them aloud with conviction – and smile.

Refer to them daily as reminders of how far you have come and what you are capable of achieving.

Here are some examples:

When we are working towards our new goals, it is important to surround ourselves with constant reminders and little triggers to help us stay on track and remain intentional and focused. Whatever you are working towards, there are plenty of ways to make sure you are always manifesting ways to get there.

Here are just a few things that you can do in addition to your daily writing activities to promote intentional positivity and happiness:

- Set a regular reminder for your goals on your phone.

- Change your passwords and ringtones to something happy and positive.

- Put a picture of whatever your goal is in your purse/bag/wallet.

- Take home a stone or shell from a walk to remind you of happy days.

- Pick some flowers for your room.

- Call a friend just to say hi.

- Don't save anything for 'best'. Wear it now and feel great.

- Make yourself a fresh cup of tea with your favourite teapot and a lovely mug.

- Sit in a lovely café by yourself for a whole afternoon.

- Use your best stationery and pens and send letters to people.

- Use all those beauty and pampering products that you were given but are 'saving' for some reason.

- Buy something delicious to eat – just for you.

- Sit down with a good book and a glass of wine.

These may appear to be very simple actions, and it is entirely possible that you're already doing some of them. That's great. If not, then now is the time to intentionally put yourself and your goals first and to live your life as if you have achieved them. Without 'feeling' your success, it will be much harder to manifest it. By using some of these ideas and writing about how they make you feel, you will see fast progress.

Boards are a brilliant physical and intentional way to build our future selves. We research what we want to do and how we will get there – and we create a piece of inspirational art in the process. Dream boards, mood boards, vision boards, inspiration boards; call them what you will, they all have the same function as part of goal-setting and personal development.

You can create a board using a piece of cardboard, a pinboard or a whiteboard. Curate materials that are connected to your goal. If you want to write a bestselling book, find images of your favourite books and authors, and headlines announcing their successes in the bestseller lists. Include images of anything that is relevant – from the type of pens, pencils and notebooks you like to use, to the desk and chair, your ideal office, the latest laptop and so on. Boards like this are used by a wide variety of people. They spark imagination as well as maintaining motivation and setting clear intentions.

Your board should be updated regularly and displayed somewhere visible as a constant reminder of what you are working towards. It sets clear intentions for what you want to do.

WRITE

- What midlife wisdom and skills can you immediately think of that could be useful to you as you set your new goals? What can help you stay intentional with your plans? Where did you get these skills? How can they help you and others?

Summary

- In this chapter you have learned about the importance of integrity and intention

- You have started to understand the power of a simple list

- You know how to write with intention and the importance of positive affirmations

13
Time To Transform

It's not often that we take time to stop, look around us and examine our life in any great detail. We are usually too busy living, getting on with things – and being distracted. But by making time to be observant, we can start to collect all the elements we need to give us the life we want and truly deserve.

Curating is the next stage of this process. To do this well, we need an acute awareness of what we already have in our life that serves us well, and of what we need to finally edit or delete.

Collect the people and opportunities that you now need to help you moving forward. Design your life your way. Don't be afraid to audit and edit again – if something doesn't feel right, it probably isn't right.

Much better to find out now than when you're almost there. You should be pretty clear by now about what is working and what definitely isn't. With your daily writing practice, you will have uncovered all sorts of things that will help you to curate and create the life that you want.

Through your writing, you should have discovered:

- How well your life values support you – and who or what needs to change
- The steps you need to take to make those changes
- The strengths you can call on
- Any challenges or weaknesses
- The opportunities that you have
- Any fears, doubts, interferences, potential threats or sticking points
- The power of list-making
- The importance of using proactive and positive words, affirmations, intentions and actions to underpin your goal-setting

Above all, you should have developed a daily writing habit that will help you write your way out of any negativity and into a new positive mindset.

CASE STUDY

Julie needed to switch things up at home and get on top of decluttering. She also wanted to work more but was finding it difficult to move forward. She embraced a daily writing routine and has never been happier.

'I am motivated and letting go! I have loved the daily journalling and writing exercises and they have really helped me. It has helped me to get motivated to sort out my house and let go of things that I no longer need. Daily writing helps you find a way to make progress – no matter how big or small your plans are.'

Julie, entrepreneur. Determined. Takes no prisoners.

You can now take your writing to the next level. Use it to list the things you need to curate your best life. It's time to create your team of champions and step into the spotlight with your inspirational ideas, confidence and plans for the future, secure in the knowledge that you have edited your life effectively, defined your goals and embraced your new-found empowerment.

Your life in chapters

Now it's time to start building the way forward and design your road map. One way to do this is to think of your new life in chapters. By creating a structure, you can plan your success and plot the activities you will need to do to move closer to your goal.

A good way to plan anything is to use sticky notes, postcards or pieces of paper to write down the individual stages you need to work through. By writing this way, you lend specific purpose to your plans. You gain a laser-beam focus that will define not only your end goal or goals, but all the stages, steps, mini- and micro-goals that you need to go through first.

WRITE

- This specific writing exercise has been designed to be energetic, dynamic and pacy. Don't procrastinate. Just take each piece of paper and write down an action that you need to take for each stage. Then map it out and look at how your journey is developing.

- For each stage of your goal-setting, create a new 'life chapter' and add headings under each one for anything you need to do to get there. Before you know it, you will have started to write the rest of your life.

As you write, you may start to stumble and get distracted, but it's important to be clear about what you are writing and why. Use the acronyms CLEAR and WRITE if you start to go off course:

- Curate your new life.

- Let go of limiting beliefs.

- Edit your life.

- Affirm positively.

- Remember to be grateful.

- What's stopping you?

- Rethink your priorities.

- Inspire positive actions.

- Tell yourself that you can do this.

- Energise your goal-setting with empowering, effective actions.

Make the most of your writing time.

Your life is a story waiting to be written – by you. Its previous chapters do not have to influence the ones you are about to write. Write the script for the play you want to act in; your life can be any story you choose. We can't go back and change the beginning of our story – but we can start from now and write a brand-new ending.

Writing down your goals by hand is a powerful and proven way to manifest significant, lasting change in your life.

Decide today that you will 'write happy' and live a fulfilled life of purpose and excitement. Use happy, positive words to clear away negativity and feel uplifted. Notice how you feel compared with when you write about negative experiences and feelings.

Fresh ideas, exciting plans

Writing helps us to explore new ideas and banish negativity. Nurture and grow your new ideas by writing every day. Use beautiful, descriptive words to define your goals and aspirations.

Daily writing is a phenomenally powerful way to unburden ourselves and work through all the challenges life throws at us. But don't focus on negativity – pay attention to all the good things you already have. Write in detail about anything positive happening in your life right now and see what comes back at you! Use your daily writing to cultivate an 'attitude of gratitude' and document everything you are truly grateful for.

Find your motivation

Look at one goal you are aiming for, or even a step towards one of your goals. Ask yourself three times why you really want to do it. Why is it a good idea? Why will it bring you what you want? Why will it change your life?

Don't worry about how. Focus on the why, the reason you want to achieve this goal. This will fire your imagination and reignite your passion for change. Think about how you will feel when you reach this goal. Visualise the change and the new life that you will have.

Small, specific steps

Good things come to those who wait, but better things come to those who go out and get them. Take one area of your life that isn't quite functioning properly and write down all the ways you could make it:

- Good

- Even better

- Great

- Awesome

Be ambitious with your choice of words. Remember that small, specific steps can easily take you from good to awesome.

Courage through writing

Daily writing should be your new best friend and your companion for life. It will always be there to help you unravel your thoughts, clear and plan. Edit your ideas and check in with yourself each day for the best results.

Find your courage through your daily writing practice. Set amazing goals, find things that will support you and write down your goals every single day.

Summary

- You now know how transformational a daily writing and journalling routine can be, and that it can be used to help guide you through any situations or challenges.

- There are lots of different ways to write and they are all helpful. Use lists, collect positive affirmations and use the writing exercises in this book for inspiration.

- You have worked through an effective and thorough editing process and you should be feeling empowered, inspired and living a life that you have creatively curated.

14
The Final Edit

Well, here we are. Twenty-one days into your new daily writing routine and you're well on your way to success.

It's entirely possible that – despite all your excellent daily writing, positivity and visualisation work – annoying and even negative things will happen from time to time. But before you throw in the towel and give up on your goals, unravel those things and why you think they happened.

Negative things like our car breaking down, or getting a cold, or not having enough money to pay a bill aren't some kind of conspiracy to send us into a spin. They are what I call 'maintenance issues' – things that happened because, for whatever reason, we took our eye off the ball.

These annoying events must not sabotage our daily writing habit, positive energy or goal-setting, but they do have to be dealt with. If you have hit a bump in the road – a health issue, a mechanical breakdown, a mis-understanding, a financial blip or anything else – just ask yourself these questions:

1. Could it have been avoided?

2. Was it caused by something I did or something I didn't do properly? (Be honest.)

3. Is this a maintenance issue?

4. Can I fix it/resolve it quickly?

5. What message am I being sent?

Write down the answers in your journal to get to the bottom of what is really going on.

When we are working hard on our personal development and something negative happens, it is vital that we stay focused, deal with it and move on. It is not beneficial to suggest that the universe thinks we don't deserve success or positive change in our lives. There is a saying that bad things happen in threes; that may be true, but guess what? Good things can happen in threes, too.

Every day for the next week, do something to move you closer to your goals. Document everything in your journal, providing evidence to support your activity. Doing this will bring opportunities to you and eradicate any negativity that might still be hanging around.

WRITE

This exercise helps us define what we no longer want or need in our lives – and what we really do want. As you start to write the new, improved script for your life in your journal, ask yourself:

- What don't I want any more?

- What do I want now?

- Add more details about how your new life will be, and what you can implement right now to help you move towards your goals.

- Ask yourself what you would do differently if you had already achieved your goals. What parts of your life would you change?

Routines and plans

To make sure that your life plan works the way you want it to, and that you achieve the goals you have set for yourself during this process, it's important to get into the habit of habits. Your writing habit is the most important. You now know how brilliantly daily writing works; it should be a no-brainer to adopt a daily writing habit.

Having routines, plans, schedules and rituals will keep you on track and help you to identify problems before they can sabotage progress. Think of it as like having regular medical or dental check-ups, meetings with your accountant, or a regular haircut or car service. Without these 'habits', things would soon fall apart.

The new writing habit that supports your life development plan must be non-negotiable. Think carefully about habits you need to adopt to ensure your continued success. Here are some ideas:

- **Daily:** Write down my goals and all I am grateful for in my life. Use 'morning pages' to start my day and 'evening reflection' before I go to sleep.

- **Weekly:** Write a weekly action list. Celebrate all my wins.

- **Monthly:** Write a monthly plan and set a monthly goal to work towards.

- **Quarterly:** Review and reflect by writing a list of all I have achieved.

- **Biannually:** Assess my progress through a free writing exercise.

- **Annually:** Revisit and reset my goals, reframe my life and review my successes.

You can choose how to react

The way we feel about something often controls our mindset. But it's not the event or situation that is affecting us; it's the way we react to it that makes us behave, feel and think the way we do.

When we are in the middle of anything challenging, it's easy to assume the situation is happening 'to us' or 'because of us' – but that is not often the case! Sometimes things just happen and we find ourselves caught up in them.

The way we allow things to affect us can have a big impact on our positive mindset and goal-setting. Here are some tips for taking back control:

- Remember that it's not always all about you.

- Press your internal 'pause button' and take a breath. See the whole picture.

- Write down what is happening and how it is making you feel.

- Write down what you would ultimately like to happen. Use this to help you reframe the situation and return to a positive mindset.

- Write down three things that are going really well, and that you are grateful for right now.

Grab a pen. On the left of your page, write down anything in your life that you feel is not working well, is causing you stress or is challenging for you at the moment.

Read through the list and take a moment to reflect. Which items do you have the power to change? Which do you have no control over? Delete anything that you cannot change; there is no point in stressing about things you can't control.

Now, for all those things that you can change, think of what actions you can take to make the situation better. They could be radical changes or small steps that will improve the situation a little at a time. Write down your ideas.

Be your own stress manager:

- Write down what you do and how you spend your time every day for a week and notice what things are causing you stress.

- Describe the stressful situation in detail. What exactly is contributing to your feelings of stress?

- Rate each stressful situation from one to ten (with one being no stress and ten being maximum stress).

- Choose one or two situations from the list and write down actions that you can take to improve them.

- Consider your reactions. What can you do in this situation to pause, reframe and return to a positive mindset?

Daily writing 101

Whenever you need a gentle nudge, some extra encouragement or a reminder – and you don't have time to read the whole book again – simply turn to these pages for some quick tips to help you stay motivated.

Instant inspiration

We all have hopes, dreams and ideas about how we want our life to be, and yet very few of us ever take the time to write them down. Those of us who do can achieve great things and make profound changes to our lives.

Something astonishing happens when we put pen to paper. By physically writing down our thoughts, feelings, plans and dreams, we effect a powerful transformation in the way we think and feel about our lives. Over time, we can radically alter our mindset and behaviour patterns, explore and process 'failures' in our past, challenge deeply ingrained beliefs about what we are capable of, and overcome seemingly insurmountable obstacles.

The great thing is that wherever you are in your life right now, you can make positive changes right away with just a pen and paper. You don't need to have all the answers before you start writing. The important thing is that you start.

If you want to unravel your thoughts and discover what you really want from life, a pen and paper are your most powerful tools. Writing is better than just thinking about what you want, it is better than talking about what you want – and it's definitely better than typing what you want on a keyboard or touch screen. Writing by hand is the most powerful way to explore your thoughts and feelings and get clarity about what you really want from life.

If you make time and space each day to sit down and write, I guarantee amazing things will happen.

The essential formula for writing success

Making space to do something new every day is a big deal. Our lives are busy and we are good at putting things off. But procrastination is the killer of progress; I urge you to grab that pen and start writing now, if you haven't already. Even small steps can get you off the starting blocks.

Here is a reminder of some top takeaways to get you started.

- Choose your equipment with care. Invest in a good-quality journal and a pen that is comfortable to hold. This is an investment in your future self.

- Choose your environment. Find a peaceful place, make yourself comfortable, minimise distractions and turn off the tech!

- Schedule in daily writing time. Even ten minutes a day will help. Choose a time when you won't be interrupted and you're well-rested and alert.

- Struggling to focus? Try writing in a public place like your local cafe. Venturing out can make you less inclined to succumb to your inner critic.

- Use mental triggers. If you usually stop for a coffee at 10.30am, make that your time to write.

Blast procrastination out of the water

You're up bright and early, sitting at your writing desk with a cup of coffee, pen in hand, ready to get started. And your mind goes blank. You cannot think of a single thing to write. A voice inside your head starts to tell you can't do this, it's a waste of time, you have nothing worthwhile to say.

Trust me: you're definitely not the first person to stare at an empty page wondering if anything you have to say is good enough. It can be tough to lower the volume on those negative thoughts and make that first mark. Sometimes we need to set ourselves some parameters and then go for it without thinking too much. If you're stuck and starting to doubt yourself, try the exercise below to get you into your flow. It's deceptively simple. You might be surprised at what you produce but whatever you write, by the end of the exercise you will have filled one page.

One page, ten minutes

Take a blank piece of paper and set a timer for ten minutes. Write, doodle, draw or scribble the first things that come into your mind. Don't think too much. Don't worry about neatness or order – just let it flow. Keep going until you have filled the page, then look at what you produced and notice how you feel about it.

Get your writing groove on

Freestyle it. Write what comes to mind immediately – likes, dislikes, thoughts, feelings, plans – but don't overthink. Just write down:

- All the things you are grateful for and that make you happy.

- Your goals, every day.

- Your inspiration. Collect and curate positive affirmations, quotes and sayings. Write them down often.

- Lists. Use them to brainstorm, explore options, organise your thoughts, make plans and focus your mind.

Remember to read and review. Each week, look back over your journal entries to see how far you have come and then make plans for the next seven days.

WRITING IS A WAY TO:

- Wonder about the future
- Re-frame past experiences
- Investigate new ideas
- Take time for YOU

Energise your goal-setting

Have you ever asked yourself what you really want from your life? Not many people do, but by writing every day, you clear a space to think clearly about how you want your life to be. Let your imagination run free and start paying attention to what your heart is telling you.

Make your life list

Make time to write down all the things you would love to happen. Once you commit them to paper, you give them substance. You send a clear message to the universe that these things matter to you. You'll be astonished at the opportunities that present themselves when you channel your energy, focus and positivity into what you really want.

If we write in a focused way every day, we can make success a habit. Stop and think about how awesome that is for a minute. Imagine being so used to achieving the things you want that it becomes your new normal. Wouldn't that be great? I can tell you for a fact that it's possible – and by now, you should be on the same page.

Something amazing happens when we write in a focused way every day. We reprogramme our brains to seek opportunities that will bring us the happiness and fulfilment we desire – we actually rewire our minds for success. Make a commitment to yourself to write in your journal every day for twenty-one days. You can use the checklist below to give you some structure. Whatever your goals and ambitions, making time to write every day can help you to get there. Just pick up a pen and start. Who knows where it will lead?

DAILY WRITING RITUAL

- Check in with yourself: how are you feeling today?
- What three things are you grateful for?
  Daily goals: what are you focusing on today?
  Be intentional: positive affirmations, reminders.
- Free writing: one page, ten minutes. See what comes up.

Conclusion

The written word is so powerful and impactful and important. All words carry power and meaning – which is why it's so important to choose and use yours carefully, with positive intent, as you write your way through the LIFE EDIT process and towards your new story.

Words really do matter. By transcribing dreams, ideas and plans from your thought process and onto paper, you set a clear, creative intention to actively attract and adopt change. Your desires, ideas and plans are far more likely to happen when you document them, because a focused, strategic and structured writing approach lays the groundwork for success. Writing things down gives them importance and permanence.

Once your ideas are out there on the page, you are duty-bound to follow them through.

Your vision is crucial – but only if you write it all down instead of just imagining it. Whatever your vision for your new story, to make it happen you must commit it to paper. Once you start to describe your vision in detail, you create an opportunity to build and develop your ideas further. You may end up writing things down that, until that moment, you have never considered before; that is the power of writing in this way. It's why I see the people in my workshops just write and write and write. They are always surprised by what they have written and their writing always shapes their ideas for the future.

You will discover a need to write down your thoughts and to actively document the vision of your story. Word by word, sentence by sentence, paragraph by paragraph and chapter by chapter, you have worked through the LIFE EDIT. You are starting to write the next chapters of your life.

WRITE

- Take some time now to describe your ideal life – and then go into even more detail and describe your ideal day. Put as much detail into this piece of writing as you can. Don't be afraid to add to it and embellish it as much as you like. By using fabulous, descriptive words that are evocative and dynamic, you not only set the scene – you start the process of living your new life. Your future self is already starting to evolve. Now is the time to use all the information, ideas, passion and energy that you have to start writing that future.

Whatever your goal is, write as though you are already there. Write a letter to your future self. Date it exactly one year from today and start it like this:

Dear Me,

It's hard to believe that this time last year I was just starting out on this journey of self-discovery. I have learned so much about how daily writing can help me clear clutter, deal with challenges, make plans, set goals and improve my self-belief and confidence. It's been amazing!

I made plans to __ and __. So far I have achieved __ and __...

Write the letter as if you have achieved some or all of your goals; describe your new life in as much detail as you can. You are creating the blueprint for your future – so take time to craft this letter carefully and intentionally. When you have finished writing it, sign it, seal it in an envelope and put it away somewhere safe. Set a reminder in your calendar to open it exactly one year from today.

When you open your letter this time next year, you will be amazed at what has happened to you. You may not have smashed all your goals, but I guarantee that your writing routine will have helped you progress in all sorts of ways. It will most definitely have helped you overcome challenges, stay positive and stay focused.

Writing For Your Life

Massive congratulations!

You have embraced a whole new way of looking at life and making changes and you should be extremely proud of yourself.

There is no doubt in my mind – or in the minds of my many brilliant clients and students – that the LIFE EDIT works and has the potential to make significant changes in anyone's life.

In an age when we rely so heavily on digital technology, instant gratification and the constant chatter from news feeds and social media, it may seem that handwriting shouldn't have any part to play. I don't believe that to be true. I love digital platforms, but it's handwriting and my huge collection of notebooks that have given me the life I live now – a life that makes me the happiest I have ever been. No amount of writing my deepest thoughts and feelings and plans on a screen would have had the same effect; of that I am sure.

We need to get the balance back. Technology is essential, but so are peace and time and space. We need to learn to pause, rather than coming to an abrupt stop and ending up in a blind panic when our lives don't work any more. Instead of reacting to our unhappy existence and taking drastic, exhausting action, we must be proactive in analysing our lives. We must make time in our days to unravel what's going on and consciously make changes that work for us – not the changes we think we should make because someone else (or society) says so.

I urge you to continue on your journey to a more fulfilled and happier life. I encourage you to embrace the art of handwriting as a way to become the best possible version of yourself, and to live and love your very best life.

I hope that you have enjoyed reading this book and taking part in all the exercises and daily writing rituals. Please tell your friends and families about the LIFE EDIT – and please do write to me and tell me about your successes.

I wish you enormous luck and love as you continue on your journey.

Acknowledgements

This book has taken a long time and a lot of life to write. I am fifty-one, after all!

Thank you to my amazing and fabulous husband, Colin, and my gorgeous children, Sam and Joe, who have had to listen to me bang on relentlessly for years about the power of positivity and how writing can change your life. Carry on visualising success; I am so proud of you both!

To my entire family for always supporting me: Mum and Dad, Helen and Keith Edwards, Hannah and Darin, Simon and Bridget, and my inspirational and beautiful nieces Daisy, Hattie and Emilia – you are *all* gamechangers.

To my fabulous stepchildren Dan, Patrick, Georgina and Poppy, and of course Linzi, Oskar, Charlie, and Ivy and Vera.

To all the truly incredible human beings who have tried this process and transformed their lives by taking part in my LIFE EDIT courses and workshops. Especially Jane Yates.

To all my friends – but especially Fordy and Andie, Clare and Miles, Suzan and Andy, and Shaz and Rob, Katherine MacAlister, Kathryn Raybould, Lisa, Rebecca, Shelagh and Vicky, Steve and Jo, Sophie Dale, Fiona Leslie and Annie, Rowan and Lily, and Martin. Thanks to Sobia and John for putting up with all my ideas!

And to Marianne – you, my dear, are a legend!

To Suzan, Chris, Nic and Patsy for taking precious time out of their busy lives to read the draft.

A special thank you to The Community Media Group in Oxford because that is where this all began. Particular thanks to Janet Pavelin and John Charlton, and to all the volunteers I have trained and the community groups I have worked with across Oxfordshire, Wiltshire, Berkshire and London. Thanks also to Aziz Halime at Thames Valley CRC, and to all the fantastic people I worked with at Thames Valley Police – Karen, Victoria, Laura, Natalie, Lucy, Alice and Amy to name just a few – without realising it you contributed massively to my passion for positive personal development!

About ten years ago, I read a book that changed my life – although at the time I had no idea how profound that change would be. The book is called *Love Life, Live Life* and is written by Sue Stone (www.suestone.com), an amazing and inspiring person who turned her own life around and has since transformed the lives of thousands of people across the world.

I would not be where I am today if I hadn't read that book, so this book and my new life both owe a huge amount to Sue. Thank you, Sue, for sharing your story and helping me to write mine.

And to Lucy, Kate, Alison and everyone at Rethink Press for getting this book out of my head and onto the shelves.

Sarah x

The Author

Sarah Adams is the creator of the LIFE EDIT personal development programme, and a practising personal development coach, journalist and lecturer.

Her workshops and award-winning coaching programme are based on the power of writing and have the ability to create transformational successes. By using structured daily writing and journalling practices, Sarah has helped people achieve ambitious and life-changing goals that they thought were entirely beyond their reach.

Sarah has always loved writing and wanted to be a journalist from the age of ten but was told she probably would never achieve that goal because she wasn't clever enough. Refusing to give in, she bombarded newspapers and magazines with endless letters until eventually the editor of a small local free newspaper called *The Aylesbury Plus* got so worn-down, he offered her a job as a trainee reporter.

During her thirty-year career in journalism, Sarah worked for local, regional and national newspapers, magazines and in national television on prime time entertainment shows. Sarah then returned to regional journalism in Oxford and worked as a fashion and beauty and business writer while also running her own public relations consultancy supporting women in business.

A spell as a manager in corporate communications gave Sarah an insight into personal and professional development and mentoring. This developed when she worked with a community media project supporting groups of volunteers in challenging communities through the power of writing. Sarah then created and delivered a personal development course that used handwriting and journalling. She continues to deliver this training, as well as coaching and personal development programmes, in workshops and one-to-one client sessions. She also gives talks and, of course, writes.

Sarah lives in Oxfordshire with her husband Colin and between them they have six children. Her latest LIFE EDITOR blog posts are available at www.sarahadams.me.uk

You can contact Sarah at:

⊕ hello@sarahadams.me.uk

Printed in Great Britain
by Amazon

20667870R00108